NO IMMEDIATE LOYALTY

Name, Image, Likeness:
A Game Changer in High School
and College Sports

Mike Ross

No Immediate Loyalty – Name, Image, Likeness: A Game Changer in High School and College Sports

Copyright 2025 – Mike Ross

All rights reserved.

Printed in the United States of America

No part of this book may be used or reproduced, stored in a retrieval system, or transmitted in any form or by any means, electronic, mechanical, photocopying, recording, or otherwise, without the prior written permission of the author except in the case of brief quotations embodied in critical articles or reviews.

Paperback Edition ISBN – 978-1-949802-50-4

Published by Black Pawn Press

FIRST EDITION

Preface

Welcome to the era where loyalty is no longer a one-way street. The world of high school and college sports has been turned upside down, and at the center of it all is NIL - Name, Image, and Likeness. Athletes are no longer just chasing dreams on the field; they're chasing opportunities off of it. And in this new world, the rules of the game are simple: adapt, evolve, and thrive.

No Immediate Loyalty isn't just the theme of this book - it's the reality of the NIL revolution. Gone are the days when athletes stayed tied to one school, one coach, or one brand. Today, it's about options. It's about leveraging every opportunity to build your brand, monetize your talent, and secure your future. And honestly? That's how it should be.

This is the playbook for navigating a sports world where loyalty is fleeting, and success belongs to those who are bold enough to embrace the change. NIL has unleashed a wave of empowerment. Finally, athletes can earn what they're worth - and that worth is skyrocketing. From endorsement deals and social media sponsorships to transfer portal moves that double as career power plays, athletes are rewriting the rules.

But let's be real: the NIL landscape is as thrilling as it is overwhelming. The U.S. Government is stepping in to create a level playing field. The IRS is auditing athletes who don't realize free sneakers count as taxable income. Coaches are juggling rosters in a transfer portal frenzy. Wealth managers are trying to make sure athletes don't blow their earnings on designer clothes and luxury cars. And families? They're scrambling to find the right manager who they can trust, knows their kid well, and has the right connections to land those six-figure deals.

In *No Immediate Loyalty*, we'll explore it all: the strategies, the stories, and the secrets behind NIL success (and a few cautionary tales about what happens when things go wrong). You'll learn how to navigate the transfer portal like a pro, how NIL valuations work, and why the right relationships are worth more than gold. We'll also pull back the curtain on how the government is reshaping NIL rules, ensuring the game stays fair - or at least as fair as it can be when money is involved.

This book isn't just for athletes. It's for parents to try and guide their kids in this brave new NIL world. It's for coaches and administrators balancing tradition with innovation. It's for wealth managers to build financial futures. And it's for anyone who wants to understand how NIL is reshaping the sports landscape.

This isn't business as usual, and it's not about playing it safe. NIL is about empowerment, entrepreneurship, and yes, a little bit of hustle. It's also about understanding that in today's sports world, there's *No Immediate Loyalty.* Athletes are loyal to their futures, their families, and their dreams - and there's nothing wrong with that.

Introduction: The Role of My Leadership

The world of NIL has evolved into a thriving, dynamic landscape, offering more clarity - and more opportunity - than ever before. High school athletes in most states can now cash in on endorsement deals, and the collegiate world has taken an unprecedented leap forward with the introduction of revenue sharing. But in this brave new world, one truth stands above all else: there is *No Immediate Loyalty*.

Athletes today are no longer bound by the old rules. They're not just players; they're entrepreneurs, influencers, and negotiators carving out their futures. Loyalty is no longer about sticking with a single program, coach, or brand. It's about being loyal to their own potential, their families, and their goals. And that's where leadership comes in - helping these young athletes navigate a world that is as full of promise as it is pitfalls.

Today, Student-Athletes Can Earn Revenue from Two Revolutionary Sources:

1. Colleges and Universities

Beyond scholarships and free education, many colleges now offer direct compensation through groundbreaking revenue-sharing programs. For example, Major Division I schools with powerhouse football programs have allocated $22.5 million to distribute among student-athletes. This changes the game entirely. Negotiating with universities to secure the best package deal has become the norm, further empowering athletes to make strategic decisions about their futures.

2. NIL Endorsements

Athletes will continue to secure endorsement deals with brands through managers, parents or agents - eager to partner with rising stars. These partnerships allow student-athletes to monetize their personal brands on an unprecedented scale, turning their talent and social capital into real income. From local businesses to global corporations, athletes now hold the keys to their financial futures in ways that were unimaginable just a few years ago.

In this new world, talent is everywhere. High schoolers are landing deals with local businesses, and college athletes are building global brands with millions of followers. These young athletes represent the leaders of tomorrow - creative, ambitious, and full of potential. But here's the thing: potential alone isn't enough. Without guidance, all that talent can burn out faster than a viral TikTok trend.

These athletes have the drive, the skills, and the platform, but they also face a maze of contracts, compliance rules, and branding decisions. They need someone to show them the way - to help them navigate complex NIL agreements, build sustainable brands, and, most importantly, stay eligible to play the sports they love.

That's where leadership comes in. For me, guiding young athletes in the NIL era isn't just about giving advice. It's about mentorship, empowerment, and creating a foundation where these young leaders can truly thrive. Leadership is about more than helping them sign the next big deal - it's about teaching them to set goals, tackle challenges, and, yes, read the fine print before putting pen to paper. ("Awesome NIL deal, but did you notice the clause where they get exclusive rights to your Instagram Reels for the next decade?")

I'll be the first to admit that leadership in this space isn't always easy. On any given day, it feels like you're juggling about a dozen roles - mentor, strategist, compliance officer, financial advisor, and sometimes even life coach. But let me tell you, it's worth it. Watching young athletes grow into confident leaders, make smart decisions, and thrive both on and off the field? That's the reward.

The NIL world is fast-paced, ever-changing, and full of opportunities for those who are prepared. But it's also a world where loyalty is fleeting. Athletes are loyal to their futures, their families, and their own dreams - and that's not a bad thing. It's the reality of this new era.

No Immediate Loyalty is the theme of this book because it captures the truth about NIL today. Athletes can - and should - prioritize their own potential over outdated notions of loyalty to schools, coaches, or brands. My role as a leader is to help them navigate this world, build their brands, and create futures they can be proud of...."**The Joy is the Journey!**"

—Mike Ross
Entrepreneur. Philanthropist. Author

Mike@connextions.pro

LinkedIn: Mike Ross

Instagram: ConNEXTionspro

ACKNOWLEDGMENTS

To the incredible student-athletes I've had the privilege of mentoring over the past three years: thank you for letting me share this journey with you. You've taught me as much as I've taught you, probably more. "The joy is the journey," and wow, what a journey it's been the past 3 years. Watching you navigate the NIL landscape with grit, creativity, and the occasional hilarious misstep (you know who you are) has been one of the greatest honors of my life.

To the parents: thank you for trusting me with your most precious pride and joy, your kids. Your belief in me to help guide these talented, ambitious students is something I don't take lightly. Whether they're aspiring to go pro, make an impact in their communities, or just figure out how to balance sports, school, and life, it's been a privilege to walk alongside them and you in this wild NIL adventure.

To the high school and college athletes, parents, grandparents, government officials, athletic directors, coaches, fans, and leaders reading this: thank you for joining me on this journey. Whether you're here to learn, laugh, or figure out how to navigate NIL. I'm grateful for the chance to share this experience with you.

My hope is that these stories and strategies inspire you to lead with purpose, blending achievement with peace of mind.

Now, go out there and crush it - whether that means landing a big NIL deal, mentoring the next generation, or just finding joy in the journey.

CONTENTS

Chapter 1 – NIL - No Immediate Loyalty — 11
Chapter 2 – High School and College Athletes Setting Up LLCs: "Wait, I'm a Business Now?" — 14
Chapter 3 – New Era of Business-Minded, Student-Athletes: Entrepreneurs and Millionaires? — 18
Chapter 4 – Endorsement Companies: Unprecedented Opportunities — 22
Chapter 5 – Trust: Building the Future of High School and College Sports — 27
Chapter 6 – NIL Valuations of High School and College Athletes — 33
Chapter 7 – Female Athletes: Crushing the NIL Platform — 41
Chapter 8 – State Governments: To Pay or Not to Pay — 47
Chapter 9 – College Coaches Buyout — 52
Chapter 10 – IRS: When Dreams and Taxes Collide — 55
Chapter 11 – Wealth Managers: Goldmine Opportunity — 60
Chapter 12 – U.S. Government: Leveling the Playing Field — 64
Chapter 13 – International Athletes: Global Talent, Local Red Tape — 69
Chapter 14 – Parents…From Chauffeurs to General Managers — 75
Chapter 15 – Sports Agencies: Cutting Out the Middleman — 79
Chapter 16 – High School Coaches: The New Balance Act — 83
Chapter 17 – College Administrators: Building the Blueprint for Success While Managing Chaos — 88
Chapter 18 – High School Athletic Director: Whistles, Budget Sheets, and a New Playbook — 92
Chapter 19 – College Athletic Director: The Ultimate Juggling Act — 96

Chapter 20 – Grandparents: NIL Game Changers?	100
Chapter 21 – High School Administrator: Finding the Playbook to Success	103
Chapter 22 – Teammates: Balancing Cheers, Jeers, and Endorsement Envy	108
Chapter 23 – Fellow Students: Could I Borrow That NIL Car for My Date?	112
Chapter 24 – High School and College Student-Athletes: Priorities, Paychecks, and Posting on Instagram	117
Chapter 25 – Sports Fans: Cheering, Debating, and Sliding into DMs	122
Chapter 26 – The Future of the NIL Landscape: Big Dreams, Big Deals, and What's Next	127
Chapter 27 – College Coaches MUST Adapt	132
Chapter 28 – NIL Current Trends and Realities	137
Chapter 29 – Transfer Portal: When Opportunity Knocks	142
Chapter 30 – It's Not WHAT You Know, It's WHO You Know for NIL Deals	146
Chapter 31 – Revenue-Sharing: The Cost of Playing the NIL Game and the New Reality	152
Chapter 32 – Smaller D1 Schools: The Revenue Squeeze	158
Chapter 33 – Ivy League vs. NIL: First-Class Education, No Cash on Delivery	164
Chapter 34 – General Managers Hired at High Schools and Colleges: The New MVPs	171
Chapter 35 – Challenges Facing the NCAA	178
Chapter 36 – The NIL Effect - Loyalty at Last?	182

Chapter 1
NIL: No Immediate Loyalty

The world of sports is buzzing with three letters that have changed everything: NIL. If you've been anywhere near a high school gym, a college stadium, or even just scrolling social media, you've seen how NIL has flipped the script for student-athletes. Once bound by the old rules of amateurism, these young athletes are now cashing in, signing endorsement deals, building personal brands, and, let's be honest, throwing loyalty out the window faster than a quarterback under pressure.

And that's the thing: NIL doesn't just stand for Name, Image, and Likeness anymore. In today's world, it might as well mean *No Immediate Loyalty.* The traditional ideas of staying loyal to a team, a school, or even a community are being redefined. Athletes are moving schools, switching teams, and chasing opportunities with a business - minded approach that would make a Fortune 500 CEO proud. Loyalty? It's not exactly extinct, but let's just say it's not the first thing on anyone's mind when there's a five-figure endorsement deal on the table.

Here's the reality: NIL has created a marketplace, and in a marketplace, everyone is trying to secure the best deal. High school athletes are transferring to programs that offer better exposure. College athletes are entering the transfer portal in search of schools that promise more playing time-or, let's be real, better NIL opportunities. And who can blame them? For years, these athletes were told to "play for the love of the game," while everyone else - the NCAA, schools, coaches - made millions off their talent. Now, the athletes are finally getting their piece of the pie, and they're hungry.

Take, for example, the high school basketball phenom who just signed a deal with a national sneaker brand. Or the college gymnast who's raking in six figures from her social media sponsorships. Or the high school quarterback who made headlines not for his passing stats but for becoming the face of a local pizza chain. (Fun fact: he negotiated free pepperoni rolls for life. Now *that's* a smart deal.)

But NIL isn't all glitz and glamour. With this new era come new challenges. Contracts, sponsorships, and public relations are now part of an athlete's playbook. Parents and coaches are stepping into roles they never expected - managers, advisors, and sometimes, unofficial accountants. And what about the athletes themselves? They're navigating a world where their decisions off the field are just as important as their performance on it.

This chapter is your guide to understanding how we got here, what's happening now, and where we're headed. NIL is a game - changer, no doubt about it. But it's also a game that requires strategy, knowledge, and a little humor to survive.

For starters, let's talk about how NIL has reshaped loyalty. It's not that athletes don't care about their teams or their schools - they do. But in this new world, loyalty looks different. It's fluid, transactional, and often tied to the opportunities available. And honestly? That's not a bad thing. It's a shift that reflects the realities of modern sports and business.

Still, there's a lot to unpack. How do athletes balance their newfound earning power with their academic and athletic responsibilities? How do schools adapt to a world where their players are also their competitors in the branding game? And what does this mean for the future of sports as we know it?

Throughout this book, we'll explore these questions and more. I'll share insights, stories, and lessons I've learned from being on the front lines of the NIL revolution. We'll dive into the highs and lows, the wins and losses, and yes, the occasional absurdity of it all. (Did I mention the backup kicker who landed a sock endorsement?)

Welcome to the thrilling, unpredictable, and often hilarious world of NIL. If you're here, chances are you've heard the buzz: athletes - both high school and college - are finally getting paid for their Name, Image, and Likeness. It's the kind of seismic shift that doesn't just change the game; it rewrites the rulebook entirely.

This chapter - and this book - is here to help you to learn the latest and greatest aspects of high school and college athletics. Whether you're an athlete trying to make sense of endorsement deals, a parent wondering how to guide your child, or a coach striving to build a team in a world where rosters change at the drop of a hat, this is the place for you. I'll share my insights, strategies, and yes, a few laugh-out-loud stories about the NIL era.

Chapter 2
High School and College Athletes Setting Up LLCs: *"Wait, I'm a Business Now?"*

If you'd told me five years ago that high school and college athletes would need to know the difference between an LLC and an S - Corp, I would've laughed and said, "What's next? A linebacker filing quarterly taxes?" But here we are. Welcome to the NIL era, where athletes aren't just athletes - they're businesses.

Yes, you heard that right. These days, student-athletes are setting up LLCs (Limited Liability Companies) faster than they're running sprints at practice. And while it might sound a little ridiculous, it's actually a genius move. Let me break it down for you - how this works, why it's happening, and why hearing a 17-year-old talk about "maximizing tax deductions" is both hilarious and terrifying.

"Why Do I Need an LLC?"

Let's start with the big question: why are high school and college athletes setting up LLCs in the first place? The answer is simple: it's about protecting themselves and their money.

"I didn't know what an LLC was until my NIL deal came through," I imagine one freshman athlete saying. "Now I've got one, and I feel like a boss. Literally. I'm the CEO of me."

An LLC creates a legal separation between the athlete and their business activities. "If something goes wrong with one of my endorsement deals, they can't come after my personal bank account," another athlete might explain. "Not that there's much in there, college is expensive, but still, it's nice to have protection."

And then there's the tax angle. "As an LLC, I can write off business expenses," one athlete might brag. "My laptop? Deduction. My travel to a photoshoot? Deduction. The protein shakes I drink after practice? Okay, maybe not a deduction, but I'm still looking into it."

The Process: *"How Do I Even Set Up an LLC?"*

Setting up an LLC isn't as complicated as it sounds, but it's definitely not something most high schoolers thought they'd be doing on a Tuesday afternoon.

"First, I had to come up with a name for my LLC," one athlete might say. "I wanted something cool, like 'BeastMode Enterprises,' but my mom said it sounded tacky. So now it's just my initials and the word 'LLC.' Not as exciting, but it gets the job done." *The cost to set up an LLC is around $750 and I recommend hiring a lawyer to do so.*

Next comes the paperwork. "I had to file with my state," another athlete might explain. "It wasn't hard, but it wasn't exactly fun, either. It's like filling out a college application, except instead of trying to impress Admissions; you're trying to impress...the government?"

And then there's the bank account. "I had to open a business checking account," one athlete might say. "The banker asked me what kind of business I run, and I said, 'I post on Instagram.' She looked at me like I was joking. I wasn't."

The Challenges: *"Wait, I Have to Keep Track of WHAT?"*

Of course, running an LLC isn't all fun and games. There's a lot of responsibility that comes with being your own business.

"I didn't realize how much paperwork was involved," one athlete might admit. "I thought I could just set up the LLC and forget about it. But now I have to file annual reports, keep track of expenses, and make sure I don't accidentally break any laws. It's stressful!"

And then there's the bookkeeping. "I had to hire an accountant," another athlete might say. "He's this guy named Larry who's really good with numbers but doesn't understand TikTok. I tried to explain what I do, and he just nodded and said, 'As long as you're paying your taxes, I don't care.'"

Let's not forget about the learning curve. "I spent two hours watching YouTube videos about how LLCs work," one athlete might confess. "Did you know there's something called a 'pass - through entity'? I didn't. Now I do. College hasn't even started yet, and I already feel like I've taken a business law class."

The Humor in It All

But let's be honest - there's something inherently funny about a 16-year-old talking about limited liability protections.

"My friends think it's hilarious that I own an LLC," one athlete might say. "They keep calling me 'Mr. CEO' and asking if they can be on my board of directors. I told them, 'Sure, but you have to wear a suit to practice.'"

Another might joke, "I tried to explain to my coach that I couldn't stay late after practice because I had a meeting with my accountant. He just stared at me and said, 'What has NIL done to this world?'"

And then there's the athlete who said, "I put 'Business Owner' on my Tinder profile. Someone swiped right and asked what kind of business I run. When I said 'I post pictures of energy drinks,' they unmatched me. Their loss."

The Bigger Picture

At its core, the trend of student-athletes setting up LLCs is about more than just money. It's about empowerment.

"I used to think I'd have to wait until I graduated to start my career," one athlete might reflect. "But now? I'm already building something. I'm not just an athlete, I'm a businessperson. And that feels pretty awesome."

For some, it's a stepping stone to bigger things. "This LLC is just the beginning," another might say. "Someday, I want to own a real company - a tech startup, maybe, or a restaurant. For now, I'm just learning the ropes."

And for others, it's about setting an example. "If I can do this, anyone can," one athlete might say. "You don't have to be a millionaire to take control of your future. All it takes is a little hustle—and maybe a really good accountant named Larry."

The Future of LLCs in Sports

So, what does the future hold for LLCs and student-athletes? More of the same, probably. As NIL continues to evolve, more athletes will realize the benefits of running their own businesses. And who knows? Maybe someday, we'll see a college football game sponsored by "QB1 Enterprises, LLC."

Chapter 3
The New Era of Business-Minded Student-Athletes: Entrepreneurs and Millionaires?

Welcome to the new frontier of college and high school sports, where student-athletes are no longer just athletes. They are entrepreneurs, CEOs, and, in some cases, millionaires before they can legally rent a car. Forget just focusing on jump shots and touchdowns; today's student-athletes are also now thinking about trademarks, revenue streams, and how to monetize their TikTok dance routines.

We're officially in the era of the business-minded, modern-day student-athlete. Let me take you inside their world, where hustle meets hustle, and the scoreboard isn't the only place they're trying to win.

The Athlete-Entrepreneur

First, let's talk about how this era came to be. It used to be that student-athletes focused solely on sports and school. Now? They're balancing practice, homework, and endorsement negotiations like seasoned pros.

"I'm not just an athlete," I imagine one student saying. "I'm a brand. I've got a logo, a website, and a merch line dropping next month. Oh, and I also have a biology test on Friday."

These athletes are taking the skills they've learned on the field such as discipline, hard work, and teamwork, and applying them to their businesses. "Sports taught me how to hustle," another might say. "Now I'm hustling in the boardroom. Well, technically, it's a Zoom call, but you get the idea."

And let's not forget the creativity. "I just launched a sneaker collab," one athlete might brag. "It's called 'Fast Feet.' Limited edition. Sold out in 10 minutes. No big deal."

Millionaires Before Graduation

Here's where it gets wild: some student-athletes are making more money before they graduate than most people make in a lifetime.

"Yeah, I signed a $2 million NIL deal," I imagine one college quarterback casually saying. "It's cool, I guess. But I'm trying to stay humble. That's why I still eat ramen sometimes. It keeps me grounded."

High school athletes are getting in on the action, too. "I've got a six-figure deal with a sports drink company," one 17-year-old might say. "I used some of the money to buy my mom a car. The rest? I invested in crypto. I'm basically a financial advisor now."

And then there's the athlete who said, "I made my first million at 19. My friends threw me a party, but they made me pay for the cake. That's what I get for being the rich friend, I guess."

The Hustle Never Stops

What sets these student-athletes apart is their relentless hustle. They're not just playing sports - they're building empires.

"I wake up at 6 a.m. for practice," one athlete might say. "Then I have class, then meetings with brands, and then I work on my podcast. By the time I go to bed, I've done more in one day than most people do in a week. And I still find time to post on Instagram."

Some athletes are even diversifying their portfolios. "Basketball is my passion," one might explain. "But I'm also into real estate. I just bought my first rental property. If this whole NBA thing doesn't work out, I'll still be set."

And let's not forget the social media grind. "I'm on five platforms," another might say. "TikTok, Instagram, YouTube, Twitter, and LinkedIn. Yes, LinkedIn. You'd be surprised how many endorsement deals start with a DM."

The Critics

Of course, not everyone is thrilled about this new era. Some people think student-athletes are too focused on money and not enough on the game.

"Do they even care about winning anymore?" one old-school coach might grumble. "Or are they just worried about how many likes their latest post got?"

Some fans feel the same way. "I miss the days when athletes played for the love of the game," one might say. "Now it feels like they're playing for the love of the dollar sign."

And then there are the skeptics who worry about burnout. "These kids are doing too much," one commentator might warn. "They're athletes, students, and entrepreneurs all at once. Something's got to give."

The Humor in It All

But let's be real - there's something undeniably funny about the whole situation.

"I had to cancel a meeting with a brand because I forgot I had an exam," one athlete might admit. "I told them, 'Sorry, school comes first.' They thought I was joking. I wasn't."

Another might joke, "I'm the only person in my econ class who has a better stock portfolio than the professor. He asked me for advice the other day. I told him, 'Diversify.'"

And then there's the athlete who said, "I just launched my own energy drink. It's called 'Game Fuel.' My teammates asked if they could have some. I said, 'Sure, but it's $3 a can.' A businessman's gotta eat."

The Bigger Picture

At its core, this new era of business-minded student-athletes is about empowerment. For the first time, athletes have the chance to take control of their own narratives, their own brands, and their own futures.

Sure, there are challenges. Balancing school, sports, and business isn't easy. And not every athlete is going to become a millionaire. But for those who do, the possibilities are endless.

So, what does the future hold for these modern-day student-athletes? More deals, more businesses, and probably a lot more LinkedIn profiles. They're rewriting the rules of what it means to be an athlete, and honestly, it's pretty inspiring.

I set these three goals for all my student athletes:

1. Full College Scholarship
2. Graduate with a Degree
3. Make and save enough money in college to purchase a new home upon graduation

Chapter 4
Endorsement Companies:
Unprecedented Opportunities

The Enthusiasm of Endorsement Companies in the New NIL Landscape

This year has brought new energy and excitement to the world of endorsement companies, as the evolving NIL landscape continues to create unprecedented opportunities. Endorsement companies are not only embracing these changes - they are thriving in this dynamic environment. This chapter explores why these companies are so enthusiastic about the new NIL framework and what it means for the future of athlete - brand partnerships.

Why Endorsement Companies Are Excited

1. **Access to a New Market**

    The NIL regulations have opened up a previously untapped market: college athletes. With over 460,000 NCAA student-athletes across the United States, endorsement companies now have a vast pool of talent to work with. These athletes represent diverse demographics, sports, and social media followings, making them ideal for targeted marketing campaigns. The ability to align with rising stars before they turn professional allows brands to forge early connections and build loyalty.

2. **Micro-Influencers Driving Engagement**

   Many college athletes fall into the category of "micro-influencers" with niche but highly engaged audiences, especially on platforms like Instagram, TikTok, and YouTube. Endorsement companies are excited about leveraging these athletes for campaigns that prioritize engagement over sheer reach. Micro-influencers tend to have stronger personal connections with their followers, leading to higher conversion rates for brands.

3. **Flexibility and Innovation**

   The NIL landscape encourages creativity in endorsement strategies. Companies can partner with athletes in various ways, including:

   - Sponsorships are tied to local businesses.

   - Social media content creation.

   - Community engagements and appearances.

   - Merchandise collaborations. This flexibility allows endorsement companies to tailor campaigns to specific goals, whether it's increasing brand awareness, driving sales, or fostering community goodwill.

4. **The Rise of NIL Collectives**

   NIL collectives - groups of businesses, alumni, and fans pooling resources to support athletes - have become key intermediaries between students and endorsement companies. These collectives streamline the deal-making process, making it easier for companies to find and collaborate with athletes who align with their brand values. The existence of these collectives has reduced the logistical challenges of navigating NIL space.

5. **Growing Financial Opportunities**

   The financial scale of the NIL ecosystem is expanding rapidly. In 2025, the NIL market was worth over **$1.65 billion annually**, up from $1 billion in 2023. This growth reflects an increase in both the number and value of endorsement deals. Companies are eager to invest in this lucrative space, knowing that college athletes bring fresh perspectives and relatability to their campaigns.

How Endorsement Companies Are Adapting

1. **Targeted Campaigns**

   Companies are using advanced analytics to identify athletes who align with their brand's target audience. For example, a regional sportswear company might focus on partnering with athletes from local colleges, while a national tech brand could seek out athletes with a strong social media following in the tech-savvy demographic.

2. **Building Long-Term Partnerships**

   Many endorsement companies are shifting from one-off deals to long-term partnerships. By nurturing relationships with athletes early in their careers, companies can secure ambassadors who will grow alongside their brand. This approach is particularly appealing in sports like football and basketball, where college athletes often transition into professional leagues.

3. **Educational Initiatives**

    Some endorsement companies are taking proactive steps to educate athletes about branding, marketing, and financial literacy. By investing in athlete education, these companies aim to foster mutually beneficial relationships that go beyond simple sponsorships. For instance, platforms like **Opendorse** provide resources to help athletes understand how to maximize their NIL opportunities.

Challenges and Opportunities

While the excitement is palpable, endorsement companies also face challenges in navigating the NIL landscape. These include:

- **Compliance with NIL Laws**: Companies must ensure that all deals comply with NCAA regulations and individual state laws.

- **Fair Compensation**: Determining the value of an athlete's NIL can be complex, especially for lesser - known athletes.

- **Balancing Local and National Campaigns**: Companies must decide how to allocate resources between high-profile athletes and local partnerships.

However, these challenges are seen as opportunities for innovation. Endorsement companies are devising creative solutions to address these issues, further fueling their enthusiasm for the NIL space.

Endorsement companies are undeniably excited about the NIL landscape. The ability to work with high school and college athletes has unlocked a world of possibilities for creative marketing, deeper audience engagement, and long-term brand growth. By embracing the challenges and opportunities of this evolving market, endorsement companies are positioning themselves as key players in shaping the future of athlete endorsements.

For athletes, brands, and fans alike, the NIL era is more than just a regulatory change - it's a revolution in how sports, business, and culture intersect.

Chapter 5
Trust: Building the Future of High School and College Sports

Building Trust– The Foundation of Success

In the world of *No Immediate Loyalty,* where student-athletes are navigating endorsement deals, school partnerships, and NIL collectives, one thing has become crystal clear: trust is everything. It's the cornerstone of every successful deal, every strong partnership, and every smooth transition into this brave new era of high school and college sports.

But trust isn't handed out like a free T-shirt at a pep rally. It's earned; through transparency, accountability, and a shared commitment to doing what's best for athletes both on and off the field. Whether it is an athlete trusting their schools, businesses trusting their partners, or fans trusting the system, the NIL era depends on everyone working together in good faith.

Trust Between Athletes and Schools

At the heart of the NIL revolution is the partnership between athletes and the schools they represent. For this relationship to thrive, trust must flow both ways.

How Schools Are Earning Athletes' Trust

To support their athletes, schools are stepping up in big ways, creating systems that ensure athletes can profit from NIL opportunities while maintaining focus on their education and athletic goals. This includes:

- **NIL Education Programs**: Workshops on financial literacy, social media management, and contract negotiation help athletes make informed decisions.

- **Compliance Support**: Teams of experts guide athletes through the complex web of NIL regulations, ensuring they stay on the right side of the rules.

- **Mentorship Opportunities**: Schools are connecting athletes with alumni or professionals who can provide guidance and perspective on managing their newfound opportunities.

How Athletes Are Earning Schools' Trust

Trust isn't a one-way street. For schools to fully support their athletes, athletes need to demonstrate responsibility, honesty, and a willingness to learn. This includes:

- Keeping schools informed about NIL deals to ensure compliance.

- Balancing their commitments to academics, athletics, and personal branding.

- Always representing their schools with integrity and professionalism.

As one college basketball player put it, "I trust my school to have my back. They've taught me how to manage NIL without losing sight of what really matters: my education and my team."

Trust Between Athletes and Companies

For companies entering the NIL space, partnering with student-athletes is an exciting opportunity - but it also requires a leap of faith. Trust is the glue that holds these partnerships together.

How Companies Are Building Trust

Businesses are learning that transparency and fairness are key to earning the trust of athletes and their families. This means:

- **Clear Contracts**: Providing detailed, easy-to-understand agreements that outline expectations, payment structures, and responsibilities.

- **Fair Compensation**: Offering deals that reflect the value athletes bring to the table - and avoiding exploitative practices.

- **Long-Term Relationships**: Focusing on partnerships that align with athletes' values and life's goals, rather than one-off transactions.

How Athletes Are Building Trust with Companies

On the flip side, athletes are learning the importance of delivering on their commitments and maintaining professionalism. This includes:

- Meeting deadlines for endorsements, appearances, or social media posts.

- Representing brands authentically and enthusiastically.

- Communicating openly about any challenges or concerns.

As one high school football player shared, "My parents and I turned down a deal that felt rushed and unclear. Instead, we found a local sponsor who believed in me - and they've been amazing to work with."

Trust in the Community

NIL deals don't exist in a vacuum; they impact the broader communities around athletes and schools. For NIL to succeed, communities need to trust that these opportunities are enhancing the spirit of sports, not undermining it.

Strengthening Community Ties

When done right, NIL can bring athletes and their communities closer together. This might include:

- **Local Sponsorships**: Partnering with hometown businesses that reflect the values of the community.

- **Charity Initiatives**: Using NIL earnings to give back, such as donating to local causes or supporting school programs.

- **Team-First Mentality**: Ensuring that NIL doesn't create divisions within teams or overshadow the collective goal of success.

One heartwarming example came from a high school basketball team, where the star player used part of their NIL earnings to buy new uniforms for the entire squad. "It's not just about me," the athlete said. "It's about all of us."

Trust in the System: Regulations and Oversight

For NIL to thrive in the long term, everyone involved needs to trust that the system is fair, transparent, and consistently enforced.

The Role of Regulators and Schools

Regulators are working to address big questions in the NIL space, such as:

- How can NIL opportunities be made accessible to athletes in all sports, not just high - profile ones?
- What safeguards are in place to prevent exploitation or unfair contracts?
- How can a standardized framework be created to simplify NIL processes across states and schools?

While progress has been made, there's still work to do. Schools and businesses are advocating for clearer guidelines, while athletes and their families are calling for more education and transparency.

Trust in the Athletes: Personal Responsibility

At its core, NIL is about empowering athletes to take control of their futures. But with great power comes great responsibility, and trust is a two-way street.

How Athletes Earn Trust

Athletes are realizing that their actions, decisions, and partnerships reflect not only themselves but also on their schools, teams, and communities. Earning trust means:

- Being selective about the deals they sign, ensuring they align with their values.

- Staying committed to their education and athletic goals.
- Communicating openly with schools, teammates, and sponsors.

As one college volleyball player shared, "I want people to trust me - not just as an athlete, but as a person. That's why I'm careful about the deals I sign and the messages I promote."

To the athletes navigating this new world: stay humble, stay focused, and stay true to yourself. To the schools, businesses, and the families supporting them: keep asking questions, keep communicating, and keep building trust.

And to everyone else: let's celebrate this new chapter in sports. Because the future of NIL isn't just about deals and dollars, it's about creating something meaningful, sustainable, and fair.

Chapter 6
NIL Valuations of High School and College Athletes

How Specialists Determine Athletes' Financial Valuations for NIL Endorsements

The process of determining NIL financial valuations for athletes is both an art and a science. Specialists, including sports marketing firms, NIL platforms, and data analytics companies, use a combination of quantitative and qualitative factors to estimate an athlete's earning potential. Here's a breakdown of how these valuations are calculated.

1. Quantitative Factors in NIL Valuations

A. Social Media Metrics

One of the most significant drivers of NIL valuations is an athlete's social media presence and performance. Specialists analyze the following metrics:

- **Follower Count:** The number of followers an athlete has on platforms like Instagram, TikTok, YouTube, and Twitter is a direct indicator of reach.

- **Engagement Rate:** The percentage of followers who interact with posts (likes, comments, shares) is crucial. A smaller but highly engaged audience may be more valuable than a large, inactive following.

- **Platform Strength**: Different platforms carry different weight.

    For example:
    - TikTok: High potential for viral content and younger audiences.

    - Instagram: Strong for visual content and lifestyle endorsements.

    - YouTube: Long-form content that builds trust and deeper fan relationships.

Each platform is assigned a dollar value based as per follower or engagement, depending on industry trends.

B. Athletic Performance

Specialists consider the athlete's performance on the field or court, which impacts marketability:

- **Sport-Specific Metrics**: Stats like touchdowns, points per game, goals scored, or medals won are critical.

- **Level of Competition**: Athletes in Power 5 college conferences or elite high school programs often have higher valuations due to greater visibility.

- **Awards and Recognition**: Winning honors like MVP awards, All - American status, or participation in high - profile events (e.g., March Madness, College Football Playoff) can significantly boost valuations.

C. Market Size and Fan Base

The size and passion of an athlete's fan base play a significant role:

- **Local vs. National Appeal**: Athletes in smaller markets may have strong local endorsement opportunities, while those with national appeal can command larger, more lucrative deals.

- **School or Team Brand**: Athletes at schools with large alumni networks and strong traditions (e.g., Alabama football, Duke basketball) often have higher valuations.

- **Media Coverage**: Athletes who receive consistent media attention or play in televised games gain more exposure, increasing their value.

D. Demographics and Target Audience

Brands look for athletes who appeal to specific demographics. Specialists analyze:

- **Age and Gender**: For example, an athlete with a young, diverse following may be more appealing to brands targeting Gen Z consumers.

- **Geographic Reach**: Athletes with international appeal (e.g., Olympic athletes or those with global social media followings) have higher valuations.

E. Industry Benchmarks

Specialists use data from past NIL deals to determine fair market values. Platforms like OpenDorse, INFLCR, and MOGL track NIL deal trends, which serve as benchmarks for specific sports, regions, and levels of competition. For example:

- TikTok influencers typically earn $0.02–$0.04 per follower per post.

- College football quarterbacks at Power 5 schools *average* $50,000–$100,000 per deal with major brands.

---

2. Qualitative Factors in NIL Valuations

A. Personal Brand

An athlete's personal brand is one of the most important qualitative aspects:

- **Authenticity and Storytelling**: Athletes with compelling personal stories (e.g., overcoming adversity, unique backgrounds) often resonate more with audiences.

- **Charisma and Relatability**: Charismatic athletes who engage well with fans on and off the field tend to attract more endorsement opportunities.

- **Off-Field Activities**: Participation in community service, activism, or other pursuits beyond sports can enhance an athlete's marketability.

B. Alignment with Brand Values

Specialists evaluate how well an athlete aligns with potential sponsors:

- **Lifestyle Fit**: Athletes who naturally fit a brand's image (e.g., fitness brands for health - conscious athletes, tech brands for gamers) are more valuable.

- **Reputation and Behavior**: Clean public records and a positive image are vital for attracting endorsements. Any controversy or negative press can lower valuations.

C. Potential for Growth

Brands and specialists also project an athlete's future earning potential based on:

- **Career Trajectory**: Younger athletes with significant upside (e.g., high school recruits or college freshmen with pro potential) often receive higher valuations.

- **Media Savvy**: Athletes who actively promote themselves and engage with their audience (e.g., creating vlogs or participating in campaigns) enhance their long-term value.

3. Tools and Frameworks Used to Calculate NIL Valuations

A. Data Analytics Platforms

Specialists rely on platforms that aggregate and analyze athlete data, such as:

- **OpenDorse**: Provides NIL valuations and tracks deal trends across sports and levels.

- **INFLCR**: Helps athletes manage their NIL opportunities and tracks their social media performance.

- **MOGL**: Connects athletes with brands and monitors market rates.

These platforms use algorithms to calculate valuations, combining social media metrics, athletic performance, and market trends.

B. Earnings Models

Specialists often use earnings models to estimate an athlete's potential value:

1. **Social Media Value Model**:

    - Formula: (Follower Count x Engagement Rate x Platform Multiplier) + Potential Reach Value

    - Example: A TikTok athlete with 1 million followers and a 5% engagement rate may have an estimated value of $5,000–$10,000 per post.

2. **Sponsorship Value Model**:

    - Formula: (Athletic Performance Metrics + Media Exposure) x Brand Alignment Multiplier

    - Example: A high-performing college quarterback in a nationally televised game might be valued at $50,000 per campaign.

3. **Local Market Value Model**:

    - Formula: (Community Engagement + Local Brand Demand) x Regional Multiplier

    - Example: A high school athlete in a small town might earn $1,000–$5,000 per local sponsorship deal.

4. The Role of NIL Collectives

NIL collectives, which pool resources to secure deals for athletes, also influence valuations. By providing guaranteed income or securing team - wide deals, collectives establish baseline valuations for athletes in specific programs. For example, football players at major schools such as Texas or Ohio State may have starting valuations of $50,000–$100,000, even for non-starters.

5. Challenges in Valuation Accuracy

While specialists use advanced tools and frameworks, NIL valuations are not always precise. Challenges include:

- **Fluctuating Market Trends**: Athlete valuations can change quickly based on performance, injuries, or media attention.

- **Subjective Factors**: Personal brand and charisma are hard to quantify, making valuations partly subjective.

- **Unregulated Market**: Without a standardized framework, valuations can vary widely between specialists and platforms.

Specialists determine NIL financial valuations using a mix of quantitative metrics such as social media following, athletic performance, and market size - and qualitative factors like personal brand and future potential. By leveraging data analytics platforms and earnings models, they provide athletes and brands with a clear picture of earning potential. However, as the NIL market continues to evolve, valuations will remain dynamic and subject to external factors like regulation, media trends, and athlete performance.

Chapter 7
Female Athletes: Crushing the NIL Platform

"It's Empowering, It's Challenging, and Yes, We're Crushing It"

Let's talk about the queens of the NIL era: female student-athletes. Because if you think NIL is just about quarterbacks and dunking phenoms, you've been missing out on some of the most exciting, creative, and game - changing stories in this space.

The NIL era has turned the world of college sports on its head, and no one is thriving more than star female athletes. They're not just competing, they're dominating. From basketball courts to soccer fields, gymnastics mats to softball diamonds, female athletes are proving that when it comes to marketability, they've got what it takes to outshine the boys. And the best part? They're doing it with grit, grace, and a good dose of humor.

Here are six female athletes from different sports who are thriving in the NIL space as of 2025, leveraging their talent, personal brand, and entrepreneurial spirit to secure major deals and engage with fans:

Paige Bueckers – Basketball (UConn)

After recovering from injury, Paige Bueckers has reclaimed her spot as one of the most marketable athletes in college sports. The UConn star has long been a fan favorite, and her partnerships with brands like Gatorade, StockX, and Crocs have only grown stronger. Her poise, skill, and leadership make her a role model both on and off the court.

Reilyn Turner – Soccer (UCLA)

Reilyn Turner, the star forward for UCLA soccer, has been a trailblazer in the NIL space. She was the first college athlete to sign a deal with Nike, setting a precedent for soccer players nationwide. Turner has balanced her NIL success with her commitment to academics and athletics, inspiring young soccer players everywhere.

Keely Williams – Softball (Texas A&M)

Keely Williams, one of the most highly touted softball recruits in the country, is bringing star power to Texas A&M. Known for her athleticism, leadership, and charisma, Williams has already positioned herself as a rising force in the NIL landscape. Softball's popularity is growing rapidly, and athletes like Williams are capitalizing on the sport's momentum.

Livvy Dunne – Gymnastics (LSU)
LSU gymnast Livvy Dunne is a powerhouse in the NIL space, with a massive following on TikTok and Instagram. Her ability to blend athletic excellence with lifestyle content has attracted partnerships with brands like Vuori, American Eagle, and BodyArmor. Dunne's social media savvy has positioned her as a leader in the NIL era.

Chloe Ricketts – Soccer (Washington Spirit)
At just 16 years old, Chloe Ricketts has made history as the youngest professional athlete in the National Women's Soccer League (NWSL). Her NIL success extends beyond the pitch with sponsorships that amplify her rising star, including deals with soccer equipment brands and youth - focused initiatives.

Suni Lee – Gymnastics (Auburn)
Olympic gold medalist Suni Lee has continued to shine in the NIL space while competing for Auburn. Her international fame, combined with her collegiate success, has attracted partnerships

with brands like Amazon, CLIF Bar, and Target. Lee's story of resilience and achievement resonates with fans and sponsors alike.

JuJu Watkins – Basketball (USC)

JuJu Watkins, the No. 1 basketball recruit in the class of 2023, is already making waves at USC, where she's expected to become a cornerstone of the program. Known for her incredible talent, charisma, and leadership, Watkins has secured major NIL deals that reflect her star potential. She's partnered with high-profile brands like Nike and Beats by Dre, as well as local Los Angeles businesses that align with her community values. Watkins' combination of on - court dominance and off - court marketability has made her one of the top faces in women's basketball - and a rising force in the NIL world. Keep an eye on her as she continues to grow her brand and inspire the next generation of athletes.

These athletes are redefining what it means to succeed in the NIL era, proving that female athletes can dominate both their sports and the business world.

On the boys side, in 2024, I was responsible for ConNEXTions member High School Senior **AJ Dybantsa** securing a multi-million, multi-year deal with Red Bull. This was a very disruptive collaboration as Red Bull was not known for signing mainstream athletes like AJ. This was made possible because of my relationship with the CEO of Red Bull.

Why Are Female Athletes Beating Out the Boys?

So, how are star female athletes beating out their male counterparts for endorsement deals? The answer lies in a combination of talent, relatability, and savvy branding.

1. **Social Media Savvy**:

   Female athletes are masters of social media. Their Instagram and TikTok accounts are more than just highlight reels—they're windows into their lives. From sharing workout routines and game - day vlogs to showcasing their interests in fashion, cooking, or advocacy, these athletes are creating deeper connections with fans. Brands recognize this authenticity and are eager to partner with athletes who can engage audiences on a personal level.

2. **Broad Appeal**:

   Female athletes often have a broader, more diverse fan base than their male counterparts. They attract not only sports fans but also people interested in lifestyle, wellness, and empowerment. This wide appeal makes them incredibly valuable to brands looking to reach new audiences.

3. **Storytelling Power**:

   The stories of female athletes—overcoming obstacles, breaking barriers, and shattering stereotypes—resonate deeply with fans and consumers. These narratives inspire loyalty and admiration, which translates into marketing success.

4. **Cultural Shifts**:

   In 2025, the cultural shift toward supporting women's sports has reached new heights. Attendance at women's games is at an all - time high, social media buzz around female athletes is constant, and fans are investing in women's sports like never before. Brands are taking notice and putting their money where the excitement is.

The Hustle: "We're Out Here Doing It All"

If there's one thing female athletes have mastered in the NIL era, it's multitasking. Between school, sports, and now, running their own brands, they're basically the CEOs of their own lives.

A day in the life of a female student-athlete might look something like this:

- 6 a.m.: Morning workout.
- 9 a.m.: Class.
- 12 p.m.: Lunch (and by "lunch," I mean scarfing down a protein bar between meetings).
- 1 p.m.: Practice.
- 5 p.m.: Homework.
- 7 p.m.: Photoshoot for a sponsor.
- 9 p.m.: Editing a TikTok video because the brand wants "more engagement."

It's a lot of hard work, but female athletes are handling it with grace, determination, and maybe a little caffeine. Okay, a *lot* of caffeine.

What's especially impressive is how creative they're getting with their NIL deals. I've seen softball players launching merchandise lines, volleyball players landing beauty brand endorsements, and track stars collaborating with fitness apps. One athlete even partnered with a local bakery to promote cupcakes. (Yes, cupcakes. And yes, I immediately followed her on Instagram.)

The Bigger Picture: "We're Changing the Game"

At the end of the day, NIL is about more than money or social media followers - it's about changing the narrative for women in sports.

Female athletes are proving that they're just as marketable, influential, and deserving as their male counterparts. They're breaking down barriers, challenging stereotypes, and paving the way for the next generation of girls who dream of being both athletes and entrepreneurs.

And while there's still work to be done, one thing is clear: the NIL landscape is better because women are in it.

Chapter 8
State Governments: To Pay or Not to Pay

State governments are no strangers to tough decisions. Education budgets, infrastructure projects, healthcare reform, you name it, they've debated it. Most states have now passed laws across the country allowing high school student athletes to profit from NIL.

On the surface, it seems like a simple question. After all, if college athletes can rake in six-figure endorsement deals, why shouldn't high school athletes get their slice of the pie? But as state lawmakers are discovering, the NIL debate is anything but straightforward. It's a tangled web of ethics, economics, and, yes, a little bit of politics.

This chapter unpacks the challenges state governments face in deciding whether high school athletes can cash in on NIL, explores the arguments on both sides, and, of course, finds a little humor in the legislative madness.

The State of NIL in High Schools

The NIL landscape for high school athletes is a patchwork of policies.

- **The Pioneers**: Some states, like California and New York embraced NIL for high school athletes. These states allow student-athletes to sign endorsement deals, provided they meet certain requirements.

- **The Holdouts**: Other states, like Texas, was more cautious, citing concerns about eligibility, amateurism, and the potential for NIL to disrupt the high school sports experience.

- **The Fence-Sitters**: Then there are states that are still debating the issue; with lawmakers deeply divided on whether opening the NIL floodgates is the right move.

For state governments, the decision isn't just about sports. It's about balancing the interests of students, families, schools, and local communities while navigating a minefield of legal, ethical, and practical considerations.

The Arguments for NIL in High Schools

Proponents of NIL for high school athletes make a compelling case:

1. **Fairness**: If college athletes can profit from NIL, why shouldn't high school athletes have the same opportunity? A star quarterback with thousands of social media followers is generating value for their school and community - shouldn't they be allowed to benefit from their own brand?

2. **Opportunities for All**: NIL isn't just for future Division I athletes. A high school volleyball player could land a deal with a local sportswear shop, or a soccer player might partner with a nutrition brand. These opportunities can help students support their families, save for college, or even learn valuable business skills.

3. **Preventing Exploitation**: By legalizing and regulating NIL, states can ensure that high school athletes are protected

from predatory deals and bad actors. Without clear rules, the NIL market could become a free-for-all, leaving students vulnerable.

The Arguments Against NIL in High Schools

On the flip side, critics of high school NIL raise valid concerns:

1. **Distractions**: High school is already a whirlwind of academics, sports, and extracurriculars. Adding NIL into the mix could overwhelm student-athletes and take their focus away from school and team responsibilities.

2. **Team Dynamics**: NIL deals could create divisions within teams, especially if one athlete lands a big endorsement while their teammates are left out. High school sports are supposed to be about camaraderie and community - will NIL disrupt that balance?

3. **Amateurism**: Some argue that high school sports should remain amateur, preserving the spirit of competition and preventing undue pressures from outside influences.

4. **Administrative Burden**: If NIL is allowed, schools and state athletic associations would need to develop policies, hire compliance officers, and educate athletes and families - all of which require time and resources.

What State Governments Are Grappling With

State lawmakers are finding themselves at the center of a heated debate, and the stakes are high. Here's what they're dealing with:

- **Economic Disparities**: In wealthier states, NIL could thrive, with local businesses eager to sponsor athletes. But in economically disadvantaged areas, opportunities might be limited, creating an uneven playing field.

- **Legal Risks**: States worry about lawsuits from families, schools, or third parties if NIL policies aren't clearly defined. No one wants to be the state that sets a precedent for legal chaos.

- **Public Opinion**: Lawmakers are hearing from all sides - parents who want NIL for their kids, coaches who fear it will disrupt their teams, and voters who just want to know if this will raise their taxes.

What's Next for State Governments?

The NIL debate is far from over. As more states weigh the pros and cons, we're likely to see a mix of approaches:

- **Pilot Programs**: Some states may launch pilot programs to test the waters, allowing NIL in certain districts or sports before rolling it out statewide.

- **Standardized Guidelines**: The federal government could step in to create a unified framework for high school NIL policies, though that's easier said than done.

- **Ongoing Evolution**: As NIL continues to reshape sports, state governments will need to adapt, revisiting policies and addressing new challenges as they arise.

A Message to State Lawmakers

To the state lawmakers reading this: we see you. You're trying to make the best decision for students, schools, and communities, and it's not an easy task. But remember this: the NIL era isn't just about money—it's about opportunity, empowerment, and preparing young people for the future.

So, keep asking questions. Keep debating. And, please, keep a sense of humor. Because if there's one thing we've learned in this world of *No Immediate Loyalty*, it's that laughter might be the only thing keeping us all sane..

Now, back to the debate floor. The future of high school sports - and a few endorsement deals - is waiting.

Chapter 9
College Coaches' Buyout

The Impact of NIL on College Coaches' Buyouts

As college athletics continues to evolve, the introduction of NIL deals has significantly altered the financial landscape for both student-athletes and coaches. This chapter explores how these changes are influencing the buyout structures for college coaches, highlighting the challenges and opportunities presented by the new NIL environment.

Understanding the New NIL Landscape

1. **NIL Overview**: The NIL framework allows college athletes to profit from their personal brand, leading to substantial financial opportunities. This shift has created a competitive environment where athletes can negotiate lucrative deals, often leading to increased pressure on coaches to maintain high performance and retain talent.

2. **Financial Implications for Coaches**: With the rise of NIL deals, the financial stakes for college coaches have escalated. Coaches are now more frequently evaluated based on their ability to attract and retain top talent, which can directly impact on their job security and the terms of their contracts.

Coaches' Buyouts in the Context of NIL

1. **Increased Buyout Amounts**: As coaches navigate the complexities of NIL, many institutions are adjusting their buyout clauses to reflect the heightened financial risks associated with recruiting and retaining athletes. For

instance, coaches may face larger buyouts if they leave programs that are heavily invested in NIL initiatives, as these programs will often require stability to maximize their investments in athletes.

2. **Market Dynamics**: The competitive nature of NIL has led to a situation where coaches are often lured away by other programs offering better NIL opportunities for their athletes. This dynamic can result in higher buyouts for coaches who leave programs, as schools seek to protect their investments in coaching talent amidst the uncertainty of athlete transfers and NIL negotiations.

3. **Case Studies**: Recent examples illustrate the impact of NIL on coaching contracts. For instance, former UCF coach Gus Malzahn faced a significant financial hit when he left for Florida State, highlighting how the financial landscape has shifted for coaches in the wake of NIL [2]. Such scenarios are becoming increasingly common as programs adjust to the new realities of college athletics.

Challenges and Opportunities

1. **Recruitment and Retention**: Coaches must now not only focus on traditional recruitment strategies but also on how to leverage NIL opportunities to attract top talent. This requires a deep understanding of the NIL landscape and the ability to negotiate effectively on behalf of their athletes.

2. **Institutional Support**: Schools are beginning to recognize the importance of supporting their coaching staff in navigating NIL. This includes providing resources for coaches to understand NIL regulations and helping them develop strategies to enhance their athletes' marketability.

3. **Future Considerations**: As the NIL landscape continues to evolve, it is likely that buyout structures will further adapt. Coaches may see more flexible contracts that account for the volatility of athlete transfers and the financial implications of NIL deals, allowing for a more dynamic approach to coaching contracts.

The intersection of NIL and college coaching buyouts presents a complex but fascinating landscape. Coaches are now operating in a high-stakes environment where their financial security is closely tied to their ability to navigate NIL opportunities effectively. As this landscape continues to evolve, both coaches and institutions will need to adapt to ensure they remain competitive in the ever-changing world of college athletics.

Chapter 10
IRS: When Dreams and Taxes Collide

If there's one thing high school and college athletes have learned about making money from NIL, it's this: Uncle Sam always wants his cut. That's right, the IRS is officially part of the NIL conversation, and while making money from endorsement deals is exciting, it also comes with a crash course in taxes.

For athletes who were once focused on perfecting their jump shots or 40-yard dash times, filing quarterly taxes probably wasn't on their radar. However, in the NIL era, financial literacy and tax preparedness are as important as game-day performance. Don't worry, though - we'll break it all down, add a little humor, and make sure you leave this chapter ready to tackle those tax forms like a pro.

NIL and the IRS: What's the Deal?

Let's start with the basics: when athletes earn money from NIL deals - whether it's through endorsements, social media sponsorships, or selling personalized merch - that income is taxable. The IRS doesn't care if the money comes from a national sports drink brand or a local car dealership; if you're getting paid, you're paying taxes.

For high school and college athletes, this means stepping into a world of W-9 forms, 1099s, and self-employment taxes. And let's be honest: most teenagers don't even know what those numbers mean; let alone how to handle them.

Here's a quick rundown of what athletes (and their families) need to know:

1. **All NIL Income is Taxable**: Whether it's cash, free products, or other perks, the IRS considers it income. Yes, even those free sneakers from your shoe deal are technically taxable.

2. **Self-Employment Taxes**: Most NIL earnings are treated as self-employment income, which means athletes are responsible for paying not just federal income tax, but also self-employment tax (currently 15.3% for Social Security and Medicare).

3. **State Taxes Vary**: Depending on where the athlete lives or earns income, state taxes can complicate things further. For instance, if an athlete plays for a college in one state but earns NIL money in another, they may owe taxes in both states.

4. **Quarterly Payments**: Athletes earning significant income may need to make estimated tax payments quarterly. Skipping these could result in penalties when tax season rolls around.

High School Athletes and the Taxman

Today, NIL opportunities for high school athletes are growing, especially in states that allow them to capitalize on their name, image, and likeness. While this sounds great in theory, it also means that 16 and 17-year-olds are suddenly thrust into the world of taxes.

Imagine explaining to a teenager that a portion of their endorsement money needs to go to the IRS. It's not exactly what they signed up for when they agreed to promote the local pizza joint on Instagram. But the earlier they learn these lessons, the better equipped they'll be to handle their financial futures.

The IRS and College Athletes

For college athletes, the stakes are even higher. With some athletes earning six or even seven-figure deals, the IRS is paying close attention. The IRS has ramped up its focus on NIL income, offering guidance (and, let's be honest, audits) to ensure compliance.

A few key tips for college athletes:

- **Keep Records**: Athletes need to track every dollar they earn and every expense they incur. From travel costs to marketing expenses, having detailed records can make tax season much smoother, and potentially save money through deductions.

- **Understand Deductions**: Speaking of deductions, athletes can write off certain business-related expenses, like equipment, travel, or even hiring a social media manager. Properly claiming these deductions can significantly reduce taxable income.

- **Hire a Professional**: Let's face it: taxes are complicated. For athletes earning substantial NIL income, hiring an accountant or tax advisor is a smart investment.

The Missteps: When NIL Dreams Hit Tax Nightmares

Of course, not every athlete gets it right. By 2025, we've seen plenty of cautionary tales:

- **The Social Media Star**: A college athlete earning $250,000 a year from brand deals didn't set aside money for taxes. When April 15 rolled around, they owed tens of thousands to the IRS - and had to scramble to pay it.

- **The High School Phenom**: A 17-year-old football player signed a NIL deal worth $50,000 but didn't realize that receiving free merchandise counted as taxable income. The result? A surprise tax bill that caught the entire family off guard.

- **The Double-Taxed Transfer**: A college athlete transferred to a new school in another state, earning NIL income in both locations. They didn't realize they owed taxes in both states, resulting in penalties and a lot of stress.

Making the Play: How Athletes Can Stay Ahead

If there's one thing we've learned, it's that preparation is key. Here are some tips for athletes navigating the NIL tax landscape:

1. **Set Aside Money for Taxes**: A good rule of thumb is to save at least 30% of NIL income for taxes. It may feel painful now, but it'll save headaches later.

2. **Educate Yourself**: Athletes (and their families) should take the time to learn about taxes, deductions, and financial planning. Many schools now offer NIL workshops to help athletes navigate these issues.

3. **Get Professional Help**: A trusted accountant or financial advisor can help athletes maximize their earnings while being compliant with tax laws.

4. **Plan for the Future**: Beyond taxes, athletes should think about saving and investing their NIL earnings. After all, a

sports career can be short, but smart financial planning can pay off for a lifetime.

Closing Thoughts

The IRS and NIL may seem like an odd pairing, but they're two sides of the same coin. Making money from NIL deals is a dream-come-true for athletes, but it also comes with new responsibilities. And while taxes might not be the most exciting part of that journey, they're an essential part of the playbook.

Chapter 11
Wealth Managers: Goldmine Opportunity

Let me tell you, when wealth managers first heard about NIL, they had two immediate thoughts:

1. **This is going to be a goldmine of opportunity.**

2. **This is also going to be an absolute circus.**

And you know what? They were absolutely right.

Wealth managers are the unsung heroes (and sometimes the beleaguered babysitters) of the NIL era. They're here to help young athletes manage their money, avoid financial pitfalls, and maybe - just maybe - convince them that buying a $2,000 Gucci backpack is not the smartest investment.

The Optimistic Wealth Managers: "This Is What We Do!"

For some wealth managers, NIL is a dream come true. Helping young athletes navigate their first taste of financial freedom? That's right in their wheelhouse.

"This is exactly why I got into this business," one wealth manager told me. "I love working with young clients, teaching them how to manage their money, and setting them up for long-term success. NIL gives us a chance to start these conversations early."

Wealth managers are **Paige Bueckers – Basketball (UConn)**

After recovering from injury, Paige Bueckers has reclaimed her spot as one of the most marketable athletes in college sports. The UConn star has long been a fan favorite, and her partnerships with brands like Gatorade, StockX, and Crocs have only grown stronger. Her poise, skill, and leadership make her a role model both on and off the court.

Wealth Mangers are a integral part to managing my student athletes. I introduce them to my athletes when they are still in High School. Now, these wealth managers see NIL as an opportunity to educate athletes about financial literacy - how to save, invest, and budget. "We're not just talking about their NIL earnings; we're talking about setting them up for the next 10, 20, even 50 years. Because let's face it - not everyone makes it to the pros, but everyone needs to retire someday."

My foundation has monthly ZOOM meetings for student athletes and parents covering interesting topics each month.

ConNEXTions Topics for Speaking to Student Athletes About Wealth Management and Financial Literacy

1. **Managing Your First Paycheck Like a Pro**

Guide them on budgeting, saving, and spending wisely once they start earning income, whether through scholarships, part-time jobs, or early professional opportunities.

2. **The Power of Compound Interest**

Explaining how to start save and invest early can lead to significant financial growth over time.

3. **Building a Winning Budget for College Life**

Share practical steps for creating and sticking to a budget that balances tuition, training, and personal expenses.

4. **Athlete Income Streams and Taxes**

Discuss NIL (Name, Image, Likeness) earnings, their potential, and how to manage taxes on multiple income streams.

5. **Managing Financial Pressure as an Athlete**

Address the unique financial pressure student-athletes face, from covering travel expenses to balancing academics and athletics.

6. **Debt Playbook for Student Athletes**

Educate them on handling student loans, avoiding credit card debt, and building a solid credit history.

7. **Smart Tools for Saving and Spending**

Introduce them to financial apps and tools that streamline saving, budgeting, and financial planning.

8. **Understanding Long-Term Financial Planning**

Teach the importance of planning for life after sports, including investments, retirement plans, and career transitions.

And then there's the pressure to keep up with their peers. "We had an athlete call us, upset because their teammate got a bigger deal," one manager said. "I had to remind them that this isn't a competition - it's about building a foundation for their future. But try explaining that to someone who's 19 and thinks Instagram likes are a form of currency."

The Bigger Picture

At its core, NIL is about more than just money, it's about opportunity. And wealth managers are here to make sure athletes don't blow that opportunity on luxury watches, bad investments, or a lifetime supply of fast food.

So, how do wealth managers feel about NIL? Excited, nervous, and maybe just a bit tired. But mostly, they feel determined. Determined to help athletes make the most of this opportunity - and hopefully avoid buying a Rolex until they've at least paid their taxes.

Chapter 12
U.S. Government: Leveling the Playing Field

The NIL era is in full swing, and while it's opened doors for athletes to cash in on their talents, it's also created a chaotic, uneven playing field. Some universities are thriving in this new world, while others are struggling to keep up. You've got powerhouse programs with multi-million-dollar NIL collectives, smaller schools trying to scrape together deals for their athletes, and athletes themselves navigating a patchwork of state laws that determine what they can and can't do.

Enter the U.S. Government. Yep, Washington is now stepping into the NIL arena, and it's not just to cheer from the stands. Lawmakers are actively working on new federal legislation to bring order to the chaos, level the playing field, and ensure that all athletes - whether they play for a top-tier program or a smaller school - have fair opportunities to benefit from their name, image, and likeness.

It's a big task, and like everything in politics, it's complicated, messy, and occasionally humorous. But one thing is clear: the government's involvement in NIL could reshape the future of college and high school sports.

Why the Government Is Stepping In

Here's the deal: since NIL became legal in 2021, athletes have been operating under a patchwork of state laws. Some states have very athlete - friendly NIL laws, allowing high school and college athletes to sign deals with minimal restrictions. Other states are more restrictive, creating disparities between athletes depending on where they play.

For example, a high school quarterback in one state might be able to sign a six-figure NIL deal with a national brand, while a similarly talented quarterback in a neighboring state is barred from doing the same. At the college level, schools in NIL-friendly states have a recruiting edge, attracting top athletes who want to maximize their earning potential.

These discrepancies have led to calls for a unified, federal NIL framework - one set of rules that applies to all athletes, regardless of where they live or play. And now, in 2025, Congress is taking action.

What the Government Wants to Do

The proposed federal NIL legislation aims to address several key issues:

1. **Standardized Rules**: A federal law would create a consistent set of NIL guidelines for all athletes, eliminating the confusion caused by varying state laws. This means that athletes in California and Florida would operate under the same rules as those in Texas or Ohio.

2. **Transparency in Deals**: The government wants to ensure that NIL agreements are transparent and fair. This includes requiring athletes to disclose their deals to their schools and providing oversight to prevent exploitation by shady agents or companies.

3. **Protect Smaller Schools**: One of the biggest concerns in the NIL era is the growing gap between well-funded programs and smaller schools. Federal legislation could include provisions to ensure that athletes at less wealthy schools still have opportunities to benefit from NIL, perhaps through revenue-sharing models or through collective bargaining agreements.

4. **Protect Athletes**: The government is also focused on safeguarding athletes' rights, ensuring they receive proper financial education, and protecting them from predatory contracts.

5. **Address Pay-for-Play Concerns**: One of the thorniest issues in the NIL debate is the line between legal endorsements and pay-for-play schemes. Federal rules could clarify what's allowed and crack down on programs using NIL to funnel money to athletes as a recruiting tool.

The Debate

Of course, as with any government intervention, there's plenty of debate. Supporters of federal NIL legislation argue that it's the best way to create a level playing field and protect athletes from exploitation. Opponents worry that government involvement could lead to over-regulation, stifling the entrepreneurial spirit that has made NIL such a game-changer for athletes.

Some schools and states are also wary of losing their competitive edge. After all, why would a state with athlete-friendly NIL laws want to give up its advantage in recruiting top talent?

And then there's the question of enforcement. How exactly would the federal government oversee thousands of NIL deals across the country? It's like trying to referee a game with a million moving parts.

What This Means for Athletes

For high school and college athletes, federal NIL rules could be a game-changer. Here's what they might look like in practice:

- **More Clarity**: Athletes would no longer have to navigate a confusing web of state laws. Instead, they'd have a clear understanding of what's allowed and what's not.
- **More Opportunities**: Smaller schools could gain access to collective NIL programs or revenue-sharing models, giving their athletes an opportunity to compete with others at powerhouse programs.
- **Better Protection**: With federal oversight, athletes would be less vulnerable to bad deals, predatory agents, or unfair practices.

But there's also a flip side. Federal rules could limit some of the creative deals we've seen in the NIL era, and athletes might face more bureaucracy in securing endorsements.

A Little Humor

Let's take a moment to appreciate the irony of the U.S. Government stepping in to regulate NIL. After all, this is the same government that takes months to pass a budget. And now they're trying to oversee TikTok sponsorships and sneaker deals? It's almost funny, except it's also incredibly important.

One athlete joked on social media, "If the government wants to regulate NIL, they should also sponsor my next deal. I'll put 'Powered by Congress' on my jersey."

Looking Ahead

The government's involvement in NIL is still evolving, but one thing is certain: federal rules will reshape the landscape for athletes, schools, and sponsors alike. Whether it leads to a more level playing field or new challenges remains to be seen, but the conversation is far from over.

For athletes, the message is clear: stay informed, stay adaptable, and keep chasing those opportunities. NIL is still about empowerment, and while the rules may change, the potential for athletes to build their brands and secure their futures is here to stay.

So, as we wait to see what Congress decides, let's keep celebrating the entrepreneurial spirit of athletes, the creativity of the NIL era, and the fact that, for once, Washington is paying attention to something we all care about - sports.

Chapter 13
International Athletes: Global Talent, Local Red Tape

The NIL era has opened up a world of opportunity for student-athletes in the United States - but for international athletes, the path to cashing in on their talent isn't quite as straightforward. While their American teammates are signing endorsement deals and building personal brands, international student-athletes are often stuck on the sidelines of the NIL gold rush, not because they lack talent or marketability, but because of a much more mundane obstacle: visa restrictions.

Today, international student-athletes represent a significant and growing percentage of college sports rosters. They're stars on the soccer pitch, standouts on the basketball court, and record breakers in track and field. Yet, despite their contributions, many of them are unable to fully participate in the NIL revolution. This chapter explores the unique challenges international student-athletes face, the creative solutions some are finding, and the humor that inevitably arises when immigration law meets Instagram sponsorships.

The Visa Conundrum

The primary roadblock for international student-athletes looking to profit from NIL deals is their visa status. Most international athletes in the U.S. are on F-1 student visas, which come with strict rules about employment. These rules prohibit visa holders from working off-campus unless they obtain special authorization - and even then, the work must be directly related to their field of study.

Spoiler alert: posting Instagram ads for protein shakes or signing a deal with a local car dealership doesn't qualify as "related to your studies in sports management."

This means that while their American teammates are cashing checks and posting sponsored content, international athletes are stuck navigating a legal system that's about as fun and straightforward as assembling IKEA furniture without instructions.

The Impact on International Athletes

The restrictions on NIL opportunities have real consequences for international athletes:

1. **Missed Financial Opportunities**

   For many international athletes, NIL could be a life-changing opportunity to support their families, pay for education, or save for the future. But visa restrictions often prevent them from accessing these benefits.

2. **Uneven Playing Field**

   In the NIL era, a student-athlete's marketability can influence everything from their college recruitment to their career prospects. International athletes, unable to build their brands in the same way as their peers, may find themselves at a disadvantage.

3. **Frustration and Isolation**

   Watching teammates sign deals and benefit from NIL while being unable to participate can be disheartening. For international athletes, this creates a sense of being left out of the very system they're helping to elevate.

Creative (and Legal) Workarounds

Despite the challenges, some international athletes and their schools have found creative ways to navigate the NIL landscape:

1. **Earnings Outside the U.S.**

   F-1 visa restrictions apply to work done in the United States, but they don't necessarily apply to activities abroad. Some international athletes have signed NIL deals in their home countries, where they can legally profit from their name, image, and likeness. For example, a Canadian hockey player might partner with a brand in Toronto over the summer, or a track star from Kenya might sign a deal with a shoe company based in Nairobi.

2. **Social Media Loopholes**

   International athletes with significant social media followings have leveraged their platforms in unique ways. While they can't directly monetize their NIL in the U.S., some have built their brands in ways that set them up for future success - whether that means signing deals after graduation or creating opportunities in their home countries.

3. **Scholarship Adjustments**

   Some schools have found ways to provide additional financial support to international athletes through scholarships or stipends, helping to level the playing field without violating visa rules.

4. **Advocacy for Policy Change**

   There's a growing push to reform visa policies to allow international athletes to be able to participate fully in NIL opportunities. While progress has been somewhat slow, the conversation is gaining traction, with lawmakers, universities, and advocacy groups calling for updated regulations that reflect the realities of modern college athletics.

The Humor in the Struggle

Let's face it: the intersection of immigration law and NIL is ripe for absurdity.

One international athlete joked, "I can outrun everyone on the track, but I can't outrun my visa restrictions."

Another quipped, "My teammate just got a deal for free tacos. I can't get one because of my visa, but hey, at least I get free refills on water."

And then there's the athlete who, upon learning they could only work in their home country, said, "Cool, I'll just fly 8,000 miles for a photoshoot and be back for practice on Monday."

Humor aside, these stories underscore the frustration and resilience of international athletes navigating a system that wasn't designed with them in mind.

What's Next for International NIL?

The future of NIL for international athletes depends on a combination of advocacy, policy changes, and creative problem-solving. Here's what could be on the horizon:

1. **Visa Reform**

    There's growing recognition that current visa rules don't align with the realities of modern college athletics. Advocates are pushing for reforms that would allow international athletes to participate in NIL without jeopardizing their visa status.

2. **Global NIL Deals**

    As NIL continues to expand, more international brands are likely to enter the market, creating opportunities for athletes to sign deals in their home countries or with global companies.

3. **Support from Universities**

    Many colleges and universities are stepping up to support their international athletes, whether through legal guidance, financial assistance, or advocacy for policy changes.

A Message to International Athletes

To the international athletes reading this: your journey is anything but easy, but your resilience and determination are inspiring. You're not just competing at the highest level - you're navigating a system that wasn't designed for you, and you're doing it with grace, humor, and a little bit of grit.

The NIL era may feel like a maze, but remember: you're not in it alone. Your schools, teammates, and supporters are advocating for change, and progress is being made - slowly but surely.

So, keep running, jumping, scoring, and thriving. Because in this world of *No Immediate Loyalty,* one thing remains true: your talent knows no borders, and your impact is global.

And hey, if anyone asks why you're not in that local car dealership commercial, just tell them the truth: "I'm saving my endorsements for the world stage."

Chapter 14
Parents...From Chauffeurs to General Managers

In the world of sports, parents have always played a crucial role - driving carpool to 5 AM practices, packing post-game snacks, and cheering (sometimes too loudly) from the stands. But the rise of NIL deals has transformed the role of parents from sideline supporters to full-fledged power players. Some are stepping up as advocates, managers, and even agents for their kids, while others are learning the ropes of this new landscape with a mix of curiosity, caution, and a dash of humor.

Parents Are the New General Managers

The NIL era has created a fascinating shift in family dynamics, with parents becoming something akin to general managers for their kids' athletic careers. Gone are the days when their main responsibilities were cutting orange slices or yelling, "Hustle!" from the bleachers. Today, parents are negotiating contracts, managing social media profiles, and even fielding calls from marketing executives.

For those who are former professional or college athletes themselves, this new landscape feels like a bittersweet second chance. Many of these parents remember the days when college athletes weren't allowed to profit from their talents. They played for the love of the game - and maybe a shot at the pros - but never saw a dime from their hard work in college. Now, as their children sign endorsement deals with sneaker brands and energy drink companies, these parents are bringing their firsthand knowledge of the sports world to the table.

Take, for example, a former college football star that never got paid for grueling Saturday games that filled stadiums. Now, he's helping his son or daughter navigate NIL contracts, ensuring they don't make the same mistakes he made after signing his first pro deal. These parents are part mentors, part manager, and full-time protector.

From Bleachers to Business Meetings

Not all parents, however, come from an athletic background. Some never played a sport in their lives beyond a casual game of kickball at recess. But that doesn't mean they're any less invested in their kids' success. These parents are diving headfirst into the world of NIL, learning about contracts, trademarks, and social media branding along the way.

For many, it's been a steep learning curve. After all, most parents didn't expect to become experts in intellectual property law or tax codes when they signed their kid up for Pee Wee soccer. But here they are, Googling phrases like "what does exclusivity clause mean" and "how much does the IRS take from NIL income." And let's not forget the parents who are now managing their kids' social media accounts, trying to decipher the difference between a Reel and a Story, or figuring out why their kid's post about energy bars needs four hashtags instead of forty.

Despite the challenges, these parents are rising to the occasion. They're proving that you don't need to have a sports pedigree to be a great advocate for your child - you just need dedication, a willingness to learn, and maybe a good lawyer on speed dial.

The Parent-Kid Partnership

At its core, the NIL era has strengthened the parent-child relationship for many families. Parents are no longer just spectators in their kids' athletic journeys; they're active participants, working side by side to ensure their children's success both on and off the field.

This collaboration has also sparked important conversations about financial literacy, responsibility, and long-term planning. Parents are teaching their kids how to save, invest, and avoid the pitfalls of sudden wealth. And kids, in turn, are teaching their parents about the power of social media, personal branding, and the importance of authenticity in today's world.

In some cases, these partnerships have even evolved into full-fledged family businesses. Parents are leveraging their kids' NIL success to launch side projects, from branded merchandise to charitable foundations. It's a win-win situation: the kids get the support they need, and the parents get a front-row seat to their children's growth and accomplishments.

Looking Ahead: Parents as Trailblazers

As the NIL landscape continues to evolve, parents are proving to be invaluable allies for their kids. Whether they're former athletes sharing hard-earned wisdom, or first-time sports parents learning the ropes, they're stepping up in ways that are both inspiring and heartwarming.

So here's to the parents of the NIL era: the negotiators, the social media managers, the financial advisors, and, most importantly, the cheerleaders. Your role may have changed, but your love and support remain the same.

Chapter 15
Sports Agencies: Cutting Out the Middleman

Are Sports Agencies a Thing of the Past?

In this brave new era of college and high school sports, one question is quietly echoing across locker rooms, boardrooms, and late-night family discussions: *Do we even need sports agencies anymore?*

It's a bold question, but one that's becoming harder to ignore. For decades, sports agents were the gatekeepers, the power brokers, the middlemen who negotiated deals and took their cuts from both sides. But in the NIL era, where athletes can connect directly with brands, fans, and even schools, the role of the traditional sports agency is starting to feel… well, a little outdated.

The Rise of Athlete Empowerment

Let's start with the obvious: athletes today have more power than ever before. Social media has leveled the playing field, allowing athletes to build massive followings, connect directly with brands, and even negotiate deals without ever having to pick up the phone.

Why would a high school quarterback need a sports agent to negotiate a $10,000 deal with a local car dealership when he can DM the owner on Instagram and hash out the details himself? Why pay an agency a percentage of every endorsement deal when there are NIL marketplaces and digital platforms that connect athletes and brands directly - often for a flat fee or no fee at all?

The times are changing, and athletes are starting to ask a simple but powerful question: *What exactly am I paying for?*

The Sports Agency Business Model: A Double Dip?

Here's where things get sticky. Traditional sports agencies make money on both ends. They take a cut from the athletes they represent (often 15 - 20% of endorsement earnings) and sometimes from the brands they bring to the table. On paper, they're working for the athlete, but in reality, their financial incentives are tied to the deal itself—and that can lead to conflicts of interest.

Athletes are waking up to this dynamic. They're realizing that in an era where NIL marketplaces, AI - powered deal platforms, and social media analytics tools can do much of the heavy lifting, the need for a middleman is significantly reduced.

Take this hypothetical (but very realistic) scenario: A college basketball star with 200,000 Instagram followers is approached by an energy drink company for a $50,000 endorsement deal. Instead of hiring an agent and giving up 20% of the earnings, the athlete uses an NIL platform to handle the negotiation for a flat fee of $500. That's $9,500 saved—and a lot more control over the process.

NEXTWin - Los Angeles, CA - CEO Roundtable - The Wave of the Future is an alternative investment strategy group for athletes turning pro.

- **NFL and NBA:** The salaries are set because of revenue sharing. Therefore, what is there to negotiate by agents? Why pay them any percentage.

- **NEXTWin** is a CEO roundtable for athletes to discuss strategy on how to invest their money. **NEXTWin** is made up off the actual CEOs of million-dollar companies. No middlemen here.

1. Capital Investor Expert

2. Commercial Real Estate Expert

3. Residential Real Estate Expert

4. Hospitality and Media Expert

NEXTWin does not ask for any percentage of the athlete's investment.

But for the majority of athletes especially those navigating smaller, regional deals - the traditional sports agency model is starting to feel unnecessary.

The Humor in the Hustle

Let's take a moment to appreciate the irony here. Sports agencies used to be gatekeepers, the ones holding all the power. Now, athletes are swiping left on agents like they're on a dating app.

One high school athlete recently joked on Twitter: "Why do I need an agent when I have ChatGPT and my mom?"

The message is clear: athletes are no longer willing to pay for services they can do themselves - or find elsewhere for less.

Looking Ahead

So, are sports agencies a thing of the past? Not entirely, but their role is undoubtedly shrinking. In a world where athletes have access to tools, platforms, and education that empower them to take control of their own NIL journeys, the need for traditional middlemen is fading fast.

For the sports agencies still holding on, the message is simple: adapt or get left behind. The days of double-dipping and taking a cut from both ends are over. In the NIL era, loyalty is to the athlete - and the athlete alone.

As we move forward in this new landscape, one thing is certain: the power dynamic has shifted, and there's *No Immediate Loyalty* to the old ways of doing business. For athletes, that's not just good news, it's revolutionary.

Chapter 16
High School Coaches: The New Balancing Act

Being a high school coach currently was never going to be easy. Between designing plays, mentoring teenagers, and ensuring your star point guard actually shows up to class, your plate was already full. But now, throw NIL into the mix, and it's like someone handed you a Rubik's Cube, blindfolded you, and said, "Figure it out by Friday."

And, of course, we'll keep it real with a little humor, because if there's one thing every coach knows, it's that laughter is the best way to survive a long season.

The New Responsibilities of a High School Coach

Once upon a time, being a high school coach was about teaching fundamentals and fostering teamwork. These days, it's also about understanding NIL contracts, navigating social media drama, and managing parents who suddenly think they're business managers.

Here's a snapshot of what high school coaches are dealing with in 2025:

1. **The NIL Balancing Act**

    For high school athletes, NIL opportunities can be life-changing. A local pizza shop might sponsor their meal plan, or a regional car dealership might offer a deal for a few Instagram posts. While these opportunities are exciting, they can also be a distraction. Coaches are now tasked with helping athletes balance their newfound "businesses" with their commitment to the team.

2. **The Transfer Tornado**

The transfer portal isn't just a college phenomenon anymore. NIL has created a ripple effect, with high school athletes and their families shopping around for schools that provide better exposure - or even better NIL opportunities. Coaches are now competing to retain athletes who might be lured away by promises of bigger deals or more playing time elsewhere.

3. **Parent Power Plays**

Parents have always been involved in high school sports, but NIL has taken it to a whole new level. Some parents see dollar signs the moment their child gets an offer, and they're not afraid to voice their opinion loudly. Coaches are finding some parents have become their kids' managers negotiating with brands and universities.

4. **Compliance Chaos**

Most all states now allow high school athletes to profit from NIL, but the rules vary widely. Some states have clear guidelines, while others are still figuring it out. Coaches are caught in the middle, trying to ensure their athletes stay eligible while navigating a maze of regulations. And let's not forget the IRS, which is keeping a close eye on those NIL earnings.

The Challenges Coaches Face

Let's be honest: NIL has added a layer of complexity to an already demanding job. Here are some of the biggest challenges high school coaches are navigating in the NIL era:

- **Distractions**: Keeping athletes focused on their performance can be tough when they're juggling brand deals, social media obligations, and the pressure of building their personal brand.

- **Team Dynamics**: NIL can create tension within teams, especially if one athlete is signing deals while their teammates are left out. Coaches are now playing the role of mediator, ensuring that jealousy and resentment don't derail the season.

- **Lack of Resources**: Unlike college programs, most high schools don't have NIL advisors, compliance officers, or legal teams. Coaches are often left to figure it out on their own, relying on Google searches and trial-and-error.

- **Burnout**: Managing the expectations of athletes, parents, and even school administrators while navigating the NIL landscape can be exhausting. For many coaches, it feels like they're being asked to do more with less.

The Silver Lining: Opportunities in NIL

It's not all bad news. NIL has also created opportunities for high school coaches to make a lasting impact:

- **Mentorship**: Coaches have always been mentors, but in the NIL era, their guidance is more important than ever. Helping athletes make smart decisions, avoid bad deals, and stay focused on their goals is a chance to shape their futures in meaningful ways.

- **Community Connections**: NIL has strengthened the bond between high school sports and local communities. Coaches can play a key role in fostering these relationships, connecting athletes with local businesses, and showcasing the positive impact of NIL.

- **Leadership Development**: Navigating NIL requires discipline, time management, and professionalism - all skills that will serve athletes well in life. Coaches have the opportunity to teach these lessons in ways that go beyond the game.

The Humor in the Madness

Let's pause for a moment to appreciate the absurdity of it all. One coach recently shared a story about a player who missed practice because he was "meeting with his marketing team." Another joked that instead of X's and O's, they're now drawing up social media calendars on the whiteboard.

And then there's the coach who walked into the gym to find one of their players filming a sneaker ad - complete with a smoke machine and a drone. "At least he brought it back for defense," the coach said.

High school sports might be chaotic, but they're also full of moments that make you laugh, shake your head, and maybe even feel a little proud.

Looking Ahead

To the high school coaches reading this: keep doing what you do. Keep mentoring, keep leading, and keep adapting. Because in this world of *No Immediate Loyalty*, one thing remains constant: the impact of a great coach can last a lifetime.

To the coaches out there: keep drawing up those plays, keep supporting your players, and keep finding ways to turn challenges into opportunities. Because at the end of the day, your impact goes far beyond wins and losses - it's about shaping the next generation of leaders, both on and off the field.

Chapter 17
College Administrators: Building the Blueprint for Success While Managing Chaos

Once upon a time, college administrators were primarily focused on academics, campus life, and ensuring that the cafeteria didn't run out of chicken tenders. Their responsibilities have expanded to include NIL management, athlete branding, and revenue - sharing negotiations.

Here's what the day-to-day looks like for college administrators in the NIL era:

1. **Navigating Revenue Sharing**

    In a historic shift, many colleges and universities now offer revenue - sharing programs for their athletes. Major Division I schools with powerhouse football and basketball programs have allocated millions of dollars to distribute among their student-athletes. Administrators are tasked with overseeing these funds, ensuring fairness, and handling the inevitable debates about who gets what.

Let's just say, dividing millions among a football team, basketball team, and other sports programs is about as fun as hosting Thanksgiving dinner for 50 relatives with dietary restrictions.

2. **Compliance Headaches**

    The NCAA, state governments, and even federal agencies have introduced a patchwork of rules and regulations surrounding NIL. College administrators are caught in the middle, trying to ensure their athletes stay eligible while avoiding any compliance violations that could lead to penalties.

3. **The Transfer Portal Frenzy**

   The transfer portal has become a powerful tool for athletes seeking better NIL opportunities. For administrators, this means managing a revolving door of incoming and outgoing players, all while trying to maintain team cohesion and academic continuity.

And let's not forget the added pressure of keeping coaches happy when their star player decides to transfer to a rival school for a more lucrative NIL deal. Spoiler alert: coaches don't take it well.

4. **Managing Expectations**

   NIL has created a new level of expectation among athletes and their families. Many see the college as not just an educational institution but as a launch pad for lucrative NIL opportunities. Administrators are now fielding questions like, "Why isn't my son getting a deal with Nike?" or "Can you help my daughter get more followers on Instagram?"

The Challenges of the NIL Era

- **Resource Strain**: Many schools don't have the staff, expertise, or budget to handle the demands of NIL. Administrators will very often find themselves wearing multiple hats, from compliance officer to brand consultant.

- **Inequality**: Revenue - sharing programs and NIL deals often benefit athletes in high-profile sports, leaving those in smaller programs feeling left out. Balancing these disparities is a constant struggle.

- **Public Scrutiny**: Colleges are under the microscope, with fans, alumni, and donors closely watching how they handle NIL. One misstep can lead to a PR nightmare.

- **Burnout**: The demands of the NIL era are relentless. Many administrators report working longer hours and dealing with higher stress levels than ever before.

Finding the Silver Lining

- **Empowering Athletes**: Administrators have the chance to help athletes navigate NIL opportunities in a way that sets them up for long-term success. This includes providing education on financial literacy, branding, and contract negotiation.

- **Strengthening the Institution**: A well - managed NIL program can enhance a school's reputation, attract top talent, and even boost alumni engagement. Administrators who embrace NIL as an opportunity rather than a burden can position their institutions as leaders in this new landscape.

- **Building Community**: NIL has strengthened the connection between college sports programs and local communities. Administrators can play a key role in fostering these relationships, ensuring that NIL benefits everyone involved.

Looking Ahead

The best administrators are finding ways to adapt, innovate, and embrace the opportunities that NIL presents. They're collaborating with athletes, coaches, and compliance teams to create programs that benefit everyone involved. And while the challenges are daunting, the rewards are worth it.

To the college administrators reading this: stay strong, stay flexible, and maybe keep a stash of coffee nearby. The NIL era might be chaotic, but it's also a chance to make a lasting impact on the lives of athletes and the future of college sports.

To the administrators out there: keep building those blueprints, keep supporting your athletes, and keep finding ways to turn challenges into opportunities. Because whether you're reviewing contracts, hosting NIL workshops, or simply cheering from the sidelines, you're shaping the future of college sports - and doing it with heart, humor, and a whole lot of hustle.

Chapter 18
High School Athletic Directors: Whistles, Budget Sheets, and a New Playbook

NIL isn't just for college athletes anymore. High school athletes in certain states are now allowed to profit from NIL deals, and athletic directors are at the center of this seismic shift. Their role has expanded from overseeing sports programs to becoming part-time compliance officers, brand consultants, and, occasionally, amateur psychologists.

For high school ADs, one of the biggest challenges is navigating the patchwork of state laws and school district policies around NIL. While some states have embraced NIL for high school athletes, others have strict regulations or bans in place. This means ADs are constantly fielding questions like:

- "Can my star quarterback sign a deal with the local car dealership?"
- "What happens if our point guard accepts free gear from a national brand?"
- "Are we going to lose our eligibility if our volleyball captain promotes a smoothie shop on Instagram?"

The answers are rarely straightforward, which is why ADs now keep lawyers, compliance experts, and a healthy supply of aspirin on speed dial.

The Paperwork Olympics

If there's one thing high school ADs have learned in the NIL era, it's that paperwork is now a major part of the job. From tracking endorsement deals to ensuring athletes remain eligible under state and national rules, there's no shortage of forms to fill out and policies to enforce.

"I used to spend my mornings setting up for practice," one AD joked. "Now I spend them reviewing contracts and Googling terms like 'exclusivity clause.'"

And let's not forget the meetings. ADs in the NIL era spend countless hours in meetings with parents, coaches, administrators, and sometimes even local businesses, all trying to make sure everyone is on the same page. It's a lot to manage, but ADs are rising to the challenge with patience, persistence, and the occasional coffee - fueled pep talk.

The Humor: NIL in the High School Hallways

Despite the challenges, the NIL era has brought plenty of laughs to high school sports. Imagine a football player walking into the athletic office to ask if his new shoe deal can sponsor the homecoming game. Or a wrestler jokingly asking if they can get an NIL deal with a snack brand because "I'm cutting weight, but I still love chips."

Then there are the parents, who sometimes take their NIL aspirations a little too far. "I had a dad ask if I thought his kid could get a deal with a lawn care company because he's 'always mowing down the competition,'" one AD shared. "I wasn't sure if he was serious or just trying to make me laugh."

These moments of humor remind ADs why they love their jobs, even when the NIL landscape feels overwhelming.

The Impact on Coaches and Teams

ADs are working closely with coaches to foster a culture of unity and support, emphasizing that NIL success for one athlete doesn't diminish the contributions of others. They're also encouraging athletes to stay focused on their education and team goals, reminding them that NIL is just one part of their overall journey.

At the same time, ADs are helping coaches navigate their own new reality. "Coaches didn't sign up to manage NIL deals," one AD said. "But now they're fielding questions from parents about why their kid doesn't have one. It's a whole new world."

The Silver Lining: Opportunities for Athletes and Schools

Despite the challenges, the NIL era has brought exciting opportunities for student-athletes and high school sports programs. ADs are seeing firsthand how NIL can empower young athletes, teaching them valuable lessons about business, branding, and financial literacy.

Some High School ADs that are sponsoring ConNEXTions Summer Camps, desire a percentage of the profits to go toward their NIL athletic program. These partnerships help ensure that NIL benefits aren't limited to just a few star athletes.

And let's not forget the boost to school pride. When a high school athlete signs a major NIL deal, it's a win for the entire community. Students, teachers, and fans rally around their hometown heroes, celebrating their success and showing what's possible with hard work and talent.

Looking Ahead: ADs in the NIL Era

As the NIL landscape continues to evolve, high school athletic directors will remain at the forefront, advocating for their athletes, supporting their coaches, and finding new ways to adapt to the ever-changing game.

To the ADs out there: keep blowing those whistles, keep filling out those forms, and keep celebrating your athletes' successes. Because whether you're helping a quarterback sign their first NIL deal or just making sure the gym lights stay on for practice, you're shaping the future of high school sports - and doing it with heart, humor, and a whole lot of hustle.

Chapter 19
College Athletic Directors: The Ultimate Juggling Act

The Expanding Role of the Athletic Director

Once upon a time, being a college athletic director was about overseeing sports programs, hiring coaches, and ensuring the facilities were top-notch. Today, it's about all that - and so much more.

Here's what a day in the life of an athletic director looks like currently:

1. **Managing Revenue-Sharing Programs**

   With many universities now offering revenue-sharing models, athletic directors are tasked with overseeing the allocation of millions of dollars to student-athletes. At major Division I schools, these funds can reach into the tens of millions, and deciding how to distribute them fairly is no small feat.

ADs must balance the expectations of football and basketball programs (which generate the bulk of the revenue) with the needs of smaller sports. It's like trying to divide a pizza among a hundred hungry people - except some people baked the pizza, and others just brought the plates.

2. **The Transfer Portal Circus**

   The transfer portal has become a revolving door, with athletes seeking better NIL opportunities or more playing time. For athletic directors, this means constantly managing roster turnover, keeping coaches happy, and ensuring that athletes transferring in or out are in compliance with NCAA regulations.

One AD joked, "I used to spend my evenings watching game tape. Now I'm refreshing the transfer portal like it's the stock market."

3. **Brand Management**

    In the NIL era, athletic directors are not just overseeing teams - they're managing brands. Every program, from football to fencing, is a potential revenue generator, and ADs are working to position their schools as attractive destinations for student-athletes and sponsors alike.

This includes everything from upgrading facilities to launching social media campaigns. As one AD put it, "I didn't go to business school, but I feel like I'm running a Fortune 500 company."

4. **Compliance and Crisis Management**

    The patchwork of NIL regulations across states, conferences, and the NCAA means that compliance is a full=time job. Athletic directors must ensure their athletes and programs follow the rules while also preparing for the inevitable hiccups - like when a student-athlete accidentally endorses a rival brand or forgets to report income to the IRS.

One AD shared a story about a star player who signed a deal with a fast-food chain, only to discover that the university's stadium contract was with a rival chain. The result? A very awkward press conference and a lot of damage control.

The Challenges of the NIL Era

The NIL era has brought incredible opportunities for athletes, but it's also created significant challenges for athletic directors:

- **Budget Pressure**: Revenue-sharing programs and NIL demands mean that athletic departments are spending more than ever. Balancing these costs with fundraising, ticket sales, and sponsorships is a constant juggling act.

- **Competitive Balance**: NIL has widened the gap between powerhouse programs and smaller schools. Athletic directors at mid - major universities are struggling to compete for talent in a landscape where money talks.

- **Fan Expectations**: Fans have always expected their teams to win, but now they also expect their schools to land top recruits, secure marquee NIL deals, and stay ahead of the competition. It's a lot to manage.

- **Mental Health Concerns**: The pressure of NIL can take a toll on student-athletes, and athletic directors are working to ensure their programs provide the support athletes need to thrive both on and off the field.

The Opportunities of NIL

Despite the challenges, the NIL era also offers exciting opportunities for athletic directors to innovate and lead:

- **Building Stronger Programs**: By embracing NIL, athletic directors can position their schools as leaders in the new era of college sports. This includes creating resources for athletes, partnering with local businesses, and enhancing the school's overall reputation.

- **Strengthening Community Ties**: NIL has deepened the connection between college sports programs and their local communities. Athletic directors can play a key role in fostering these relationships, ensuring that NIL benefits everyone involved.

- **Developing Future Leaders**: NIL is about more than money - it's about teaching athletes valuable skills like negotiation, branding, and financial literacy. Athletic directors have the chance to help shape the next generation of leaders.

And if all else fails, remember: in this world of *No Immediate Loyalty*, the one thing you can always count on is the value of a well-timed joke.

Chapter 20
Grandparents: NIL Game Changers?

Grandparents in the NIL Era: From Sidelines to Center Stage

In the grand tapestry of NIL deals, there's a new, unexpected player stepping into the spotlight: grandparents. Yes, the same people who brought you cookies after school and told you not to run with scissors are now playing pivotal roles in guiding college athletes through the wild, fast-paced world of NIL contracts. Whether they're former sports stars who never got paid a dime or proud spectators who never set foot on a playing field, grandparents are proving to be the unsung heroes of this new era in college athletics.

Grandparent Wisdom: The New MVP

The NIL landscape is still new and ever evolving, much like teaching your grandma how to use FaceTime. But what grandparents lack in TikTok fluency, they more than make up for in wisdom, lived experience, and a keen sense of what really matters. In 2025, as NIL deals have grown to include everything from endorsement contracts to social media sponsorships, grandparents are stepping in as trusted advisors - and sometimes as unofficial agents.

Take, for instance, the ex-pro athletes among them. Many grandparents, who once played in the NBA, NFL, or on the diamond, remember a time when college athletes were unpaid and scholarships were the only "compensation." Back in their day, the idea of being paid for autographing a jersey would've been laughable - mostly because that jersey would've been washed in their mom's sink and hung out to dry. Now, they're using their hard-earned lessons to guide a new generation of athletes.

Some grandparents are offering sage advice, helping their grandchildren navigate the complexities of contracts, taxes, and, of course, Uncle Sam. (Spoiler alert: NIL money *is* taxable, and the IRS doesn't accept excuses like, "I didn't know!"). Others are simply there to remind young athletes to stay humble. As one former NCAA basketball star turned granddad famously quipped: "Just because you're getting six figures to promote a sneaker doesn't mean you can skip class."

The Non-Athlete Grandparents: MVPs in Their Own Right

Not every grandparent advising on NIL deals has worn a jersey or dribbled a ball. Some never played sports beyond a spirited game of shuffleboard, but that doesn't make them any less valuable. These grandparents bring a different kind of expertise to the table: life skills, love, and a knack for spotting a scam from a mile away.

For example, who better than a grandparent to read the fine print in a contract? Grandma might not know what a TikTok influencer does, but she *does* know that if a deal sounds too good to be true, it probably is. And Grandpa? Well, he's the one reminding everyone that flashy cars depreciate and that you should probably stick some of that NIL money in a savings account.

These non-athlete grandparents are also the ultimate cheerleaders. They're the ones liking every Instagram post, showing up to every game (rain or shine), and proudly wearing your merch, even if they accidentally call it "merchandise." Their enthusiasm is infectious - and it's a gentle reminder that NIL deals may come and go, but family support is forever.

The Humor in It All

The NIL era has brought its share of challenges, but it's also brought plenty of laughs - especially when grandparents get involved. Picture this: a college athlete signs a deal with a protein shake company, and the next thing they know, Grandma is handing out free samples to all her bridge club friends. Or imagine a granddad showing up to a game wearing a head-to-toe outfit from his grandson's NIL clothing line, complete with a hat that says, "Drip King" (even though he still calls it "swag").

And then there's the social media learning curve. Many grandparents are now following their grandchildren's NIL-sponsored accounts, leaving comments like, "So proud of you, honey! Love, Grandma. P.S. What's a hashtag?" These moments of humor remind us that while NIL deals are serious business, they're also an opportunity to bring families closer together.

Looking Ahead: Grandparents as NIL Game Changers

As NIL deals continue to evolve, the role of grandparents is becoming increasingly vital. Whether they're helping negotiate contracts, offering life advice, or simply cheering from the sidelines, grandparents are proving that they're more than capable of adapting to this brave new world. They're not just supporting their grandchildren - they're shaping their futures.

So, to all the grandparents out there: keep baking those cookies, keep telling those stories, and keep being the rock-solid foundation that every young athlete needs. Because in the NIL game, you're the ultimate secret weapon. Or, as one savvy grandmother put it: "They may have the NIL deal, but I've got the wisdom - and the Tupperware."

Chapter 21
High School Administrators: Finding the Playbook to Success

High School administrators are facing challenges they never anticipated. Sure, they've dealt with everything from budget cuts to prom planning, but now they're navigating the uncharted waters of the NIL era.

Helping high school athletes manage endorsement deals, stay eligible for sports, and avoid potential pitfalls has quickly become part of the job description. And while the road is bumpy, school administrators are finding ways to adapt, create systems that work, and even share a laugh or two along the way.

The New Assignment: Building NIL Systems from Scratch

The NIL era has added a new layer of complexity to high school education. In states where NIL is allowed, administrators are working overtime to develop policies that support student-athletes while protecting their schools from liability.

These systems often include:

- **Education Programs**: Workshops on financial literacy, social media etiquette, and understanding contracts.

- **Compliance Guidelines**: Clear rules to ensure athletes follow state laws and retain their eligibility.

- **Advisory Support**: Partnerships with legal experts, financial advisors, and even alumni to guide athletes and their families.

"We never thought we'd be explaining the difference between a flat-rate contract and a revenue-sharing deal to 16- year-olds," one principal joked. "But here we are."

The Paperwork Pile-Up: Keeping It Legal

One of the biggest challenges for high school administrators is ensuring compliance with NIL rules. Every state has its own laws, and schools must carefully navigate these regulations to avoid jeopardizing their athletes' eligibility - or their own reputations.

This means reviewing contracts, teaching families about NIL rules, and, in some cases, acting as mediators between athletes and outside businesses. One administrator shared:

"We had a local restaurant offer free food to our quarterback in exchange for a few social media posts. It sounded harmless enough, but we had to make sure it didn't violate state rules. Let's just say I know more about NIL now than I ever thought I would."

And then there's the added pressure of public scrutiny. With NIL deals often making headlines, administrators are keenly aware that any misstep could bring unwanted attention to their schools.

The Humor: NIL in the High School Halls

As stressful as the NIL era can be, it's also brought plenty of laughs to high schools across the country.

Picture this: a student walks into the principal's office to ask if they can skip gym class for a photoshoot with their NIL sponsor. Or a parent emails the administration asking if their child's endorsement deal with a local smoothie shop means they can wear non-uniform sweatshirts to class.

And then there are the sponsorship pitches. One administrator recalled a group of athletes jokingly asking if the school could get a deal with a popular sneaker brand so "the whole basketball team could look fresh for home games."

These moments of levity remind administrators why they do what they do - even when the NIL paperwork feels never-ending.

Balancing Academics and Athletics

For high school administrators, one of the biggest concerns in the NIL era is ensuring that academics remain a priority. It's easy for young athletes to get caught up in the excitement of endorsement deals, but school leaders are working hard to keep them grounded.

This means reinforcing the importance of time management, encouraging athletes to stay focused on their studies, and reminding them that their long - term success depends on more than just NIL opportunities.

"We tell our athletes all the time: You're a student first and an athlete second," one principal said. "And now we add, 'And your NIL deals come third.'"

The Impact on School Culture

NIL has also created ripple effects throughout high school communities. While some students are excited to see their peers succeed, others worry about the potential for jealousy or division.

Administrators are stepping in to foster a culture of support and inclusion, emphasizing the idea that one athlete's success is a win for the entire school. They're also using NIL as an opportunity to teach valuable life lessons about teamwork, humility, and the importance of giving back.

"We had a soccer player land an NIL deal with a local charity," one administrator shared. "She used part of her earnings to donate equipment to the school's PE program. That's the kind of leadership we want to celebrate."

Opportunities for Schools and Communities

Despite the challenges, the NIL era has opened up exciting opportunities for high schools and their surrounding communities.

Some administrators are working with local businesses to create partnerships that benefit entire teams or programs. For example, a company might sponsor a school's football team, providing new uniforms or equipment in exchange for promotional support. These collaborations help ensure that NIL benefits aren't limited to just a few star athletes.

NIL has also brought positive attention to high school sports, with students, parents, and fans rallying around their teams. For administrators, it's a chance to highlight the incredible talent and dedication of their student-athletes - both on and off the field.

Looking Ahead: The Future of NIL in High Schools

As the NIL landscape and demand continues to evolve, high school administrators are committed to staying ahead of the curve. They're advocating for clearer state and national guidelines, collaborating with other schools to share best practices, and finding innovative ways to support their athletes while maintaining the integrity of their programs.

To the administrators out there: keep building those systems, keep supporting your athletes, and keep finding ways to turn challenges into opportunities. Because whether you're reviewing contracts, hosting NIL workshops, or simply cheering from the stands, you're shaping the future of high school sports - and doing it with heart, humor, and a whole lot of hustle.

Chapter 22
Teammates: Balancing Cheers, Jeers, and Endorsement Envy

In the world of sports, teammates are like family. They sweat together, celebrate together, and pick each other up after tough losses. But what happens when one teammate lands a six-figure shoe deal while the rest are still splitting post-game pizzas? Welcome to the NIL era, where navigating the locker room dynamic has become as much about managing emotions as executing plays on the field.

In 2025, the NIL landscape has matured, bringing not only opportunities but also challenges - particularly when it comes to how teammates react to one another's newfound fame and fortune. Spoiler alert: it's not always smooth sailing. But with a little humor, a lot of communication, and some good old-fashioned camaraderie, teams are finding ways to stay united.

The Star Player Spotlight: A Double-Edged Sword

Let's face it: every team has its star player. The quarterback with the cannon arm, the forward who can't stop scoring, or the shortstop who turns double plays like magic. In the NIL era, these star players are often the ones raking in the big endorsement deals. Think luxury cars, sneaker lines, and energy drink partnerships plastered all over social media.

For some teammates, this success feels like a win for the team. After all, when one player gets recognized, it often shines a spotlight on the entire program. But for others, it can bring up feelings of jealousy or frustration, especially when the attention feels one-sided.

Take the offensive lineman, for example. He's in the trenches every game, protecting the quarterback's blindside, but it's the QB who's on billboards and magazine covers. Or the defensive stopper who locks down the opposing team's best player, only to see their teammate's dunk go viral on TikTok. As one anonymous college athlete put it: "I'm happy for him, but man, I'd love a free car too."

The Humor of It: NIL Locker Room Banter

Luckily, athletes have a way of diffusing tension - with humor. In locker rooms across the country, NIL deals have become a source of endless jokes and good-natured ribbing.

Imagine a teammate walking in with a fresh pair of NIL - sponsored sneakers, only to hear someone shout, "Oh, I see how it is - you're too good for team-issued gear now?" Or a player showing up to practice in their new NIL-branded sweat suit, only to be jokingly asked if they're charging for autographs now.

And then there are the running gags about endorsement deals that *didn't* happen. "Hey, if you get a deal with a chicken wing company, you better share," one teammate might quip. Or, "When's the NIL deal for benchwarmers coming out? I'm ready to sign!" These jokes help keep things light and remind everyone that, at the end of the day, they're in this together.

The Real Conversations: Addressing the Elephant in the Room

While humor helps, NIL dynamics have also sparked deeper conversations among teammates about fairness, equity, and the nature of success. Coaches and athletic departments are increasingly stepping in to mediate and educate players on how to handle these situations.

Many teams now hold workshops on financial literacy and NIL education, making it clear that one player's success doesn't diminish another's value. Coaches emphasize the importance of focusing on collective goals such as winning games, building chemistry, and supporting each other - over individual accolades.

And for the players earning big money, there's often an unspoken responsibility to stay humble and grounded. As one college basketball star said: "Yeah, I've got a deal with a clothing brand, but I wouldn't have it without my teammates. They're the ones making me look good out there."

The Silver Lining: Opportunities for Everyone

Here's the good news: the NIL era isn't just about star players. While it's true that quarterbacks and scorers often get the biggest deals, there's room for everyone to benefit.

In 2025, NIL opportunities have expanded to include niche markets and creative collaborations. The backup goalie that's a whiz at video games? He's streaming on Twitch with sponsorship deals. The defensive specialist who's an amazing cook? She's partnered with a meal prep company. The walk-on who's hilarious on TikTok? She's got a deal with a comedy app.

Teammates are also finding ways to lift each other up. Some star players use their platforms to spotlight their less-recognized teammates, tagging them in posts or sharing credit for big wins. Others are pooling their resources to create team-wide NIL opportunities, such as joint social media campaigns or shared endorsement deals.

The Big Picture: Team First, Always

At the heart of it all, the NIL era is teaching athletes valuable lessons about teamwork, communication, and gratitude. Yes, there will be moments of tension and envy, but there will also be moments of pride and solidarity.

Teammates are learning to celebrate each other's wins - whether it's a game-winning shot or a new NIL deal. They're realizing that while individual success is great, it's the collective effort that truly matters. And they're finding ways to support each other, both on and off the field, because that's what being part of a team is all about.

So, to the athletes navigating NIL dynamics in 2025: keep cheering for each other, keep cracking jokes, and keep chasing your dreams. Because at the end of the day, the only thing better than winning is winning *together*. And hey, if your teammate gets a free car, maybe they'll give you a ride to practice.

Chapter 23
Fellow Students: *"Could I Borrow That NIL Car for My Date?"*

The NIL era isn't just changing the lives of high school and college athletes - it's also shaking up the world of their classmates. For the regular students walking the same hallways and sitting in the same lecture halls as their NIL-earning peers, the experience is a mix of awe, curiosity, and, occasionally, some lighthearted envy.

After all, it's not every day that your roommate walks into your dorm with a six-figure endorsement deal or your lab partner casually drops that they're headed to a photoshoot for a protein bar company after class. So how do non-athlete students really feel about their peers cashing in on NIL? Let's take a closer look.

The Supporters: "Good for Them!"

A large number of regular students are fully supportive of their athlete classmates making money through NIL. These are the students who recognize the hard work, long hours, and sacrifices that go into being a student-athlete.

"Honestly, they deserve it," one student might say. "If I had to wake up at 5 AM for practice every day and still keep up with classes, I'd want to get paid too."

For these students, seeing their peers succeed is exciting, even inspiring. They're the ones hyping up their athlete friends on social media, liking every sponsored post, and proudly saying, "Yeah, I know her! She's in my econ class!"

The Curious Observers: "How Does This Even Work?"

Then there's the group of students who are simply fascinated by the NIL process. They might not fully understand how endorsement deals work or why certain athletes are getting paid, but they're eager to learn.

"Wait, so the quarterback gets paid for posting about energy drinks?" one student might ask. "Do they send him free drinks too? Can I get one?"

These students are the ones asking questions in the dining hall, reading up on NIL news, and maybe even brainstorming ways they can get in on the action. ("Do you think I could get an endorsement deal for being top of the class in chemistry?")

The Envious (But Still Kind of Supportive): "Must Be Nice..."

Of course, there's a small subset of students who can't help but feel a twinge of envy when their athlete classmates start raking in the cash.

"Wait, she gets a free car just for playing volleyball? I've been working 20 hours a week at the campus coffee shop, and I can barely afford gas," one student might joke.

But even these students usually come around. After all, it's hard to stay mad when you see how much effort athletes put into balancing sports, school, and now, their NIL responsibilities. And who knows?

Maybe their athlete friend will offer them a ride in that NIL-sponsored car.

The Humor: NIL and Campus Life

The NIL era has also brought plenty of humor to college and high school campuses. Imagine walking into math class and seeing your classmate on a billboard for a local gym. Or spotting your lab partner on Instagram promoting a new brand of headphones.

Students have also taken to joking about NIL deals that don't exist (but probably should). "If the cafeteria sponsored an athlete, who do you think it'd be?" one student might ask. Or, "Do you think the soccer team could get a deal with a laundry detergent brand? They'd make bank."

And then there are the memes. Oh, the memes. Whether it's poking fun at teammates endorsing competing brands or joking about who deserves an NIL deal for carrying the group project, students have found endless ways to keep the mood light.

The Impact on Campus Culture

Beyond the jokes and curiosity, the NIL era has had a positive impact on campus culture. It's brought more attention to athletics, with students rallying around their peers not just as athletes but as budding entrepreneurs.

Some regular students have even found ways to collaborate with their NIL-earning classmates. Graphic design majors are creating logos for athlete brands. Marketing students are helping athletes manage their social media accounts. And aspiring videographers are producing highlight reels and promotional videos.

In many ways, NIL has fostered a sense of community and creativity; with students working together to help their peers succeed.

The Future: Dreaming Big

"Seeing my roommate land an NIL deal is actually kind of inspiring," one student said. "It makes me want to figure out how to turn my passion into something bigger too."

And who knows? Maybe the next big NIL star isn't an athlete at all - maybe it's the student who figures out how to help their peers navigate this new world.

The Big Picture: Students in the NIL Era

At the end of the day, the NIL era has brought a mix of admiration, curiosity, and humor to campuses across the country. Regular students may not be signing endorsement deals, but they're cheering on their athlete classmates, collaborating on creative projects, and finding inspiration in their peers' success.

So, to the regular students out there: keep supporting your athlete friends. Keep asking questions. And hey, maybe keep dropping hints about wanting a ride in that NIL-sponsored car. Because the beauty of the NIL era is that it's about more than just money - it's about opportunity, growth, and showing what's possible when hard work meets the right moment.

And to the athletes: don't forget to share those free protein bars, okay?

Chapter 24
High School and College Athletes:
Priorities, Paychecks, and Posting on Instagram

Student-athletes in high school and college are living in a world their predecessors could only dream of. Thanks to the NIL revolution, these young athletes can profit from their talents, whether it's signing endorsement deals, running social media campaigns, or even launching their own clothing lines.

But with these opportunities come new responsibilities and shifting priorities. Between practice, schoolwork, and now managing NIL opportunities, today's student-athletes are busier than ever. They're navigating everything from brand partnerships to financial planning, all while staying focused on their goals - both on and off the field.

Priority #1: Balancing School, Sports, and NIL

For high school and college athletes, the top priority is still the same as it's always been: finding a balance between academics and athletics. But now, NIL has added a third layer to the juggling act.

Athletes are learning how to manage their time more effectively than ever, squeezing NIL commitments into already packed schedules. A typical day might look something like this:

- **6:00 AM**: Morning practice.
- **8:00 AM**: Classes and homework.
- **3:00 PM**: Afternoon practice or game prep.

- **6:00 PM**: A quick call with their NIL agent or sponsor.
- **8:00 PM**: Posting a sponsored TikTok before hitting the books again.

"It's like having a part-time job on top of everything else," one college basketball player said. "Except instead of flipping burgers, I'm flipping merch on Instagram."

For high school athletes, the challenge is even greater, as they're often balancing NIL commitments with curfews, homework assignments, and the occasional family dinner.

Priority #2: Staying Focused on Long-Term Goals

While NIL opportunities are exciting, most athletes understand that their long-term success depends on more than just endorsement deals. For many, the ultimate goal is still earning a college scholarship, excelling in their sport, or preparing for a professional career.

"I remind myself every day that NIL is just a bonus," one high school football player shared. "My main focus is getting better on the field and in the classroom. The rest will come."

In college, athletes are thinking about life after graduation, whether that means going pro, pursuing a career in their chosen field, or even starting their own business. NIL has opened up new doors, but it's also taught athletes the importance of planning for the future.

Priority #3: Protecting Their Brand

In the NIL era, athletes are more than just players - they're brands. High school and college athletes are learning how to present themselves professionally, build their social media presence, and choose partnerships that align with their values.

This means being selective about which deals they accept. "I turned down a sponsorship with an energy drink company because it didn't feel authentic to me," one college soccer player said. "I want my brand to reflect who I really am."

Athletes are also becoming more aware of their social media activity, knowing that every post, comment, and like can impact their reputation - and their NIL opportunities.

"I used to post whatever came to mind," a high school basketball player admitted. "Now I think twice before hitting 'send.'"

Priority #4: Learning Financial Literacy

For many student-athletes, NIL is their first experience with managing significant amounts of money. Whether it's a few hundred dollars from a local sponsorship or a six-figure deal with a national brand, athletes are learning how to handle their earnings wisely.

Schools and families are stepping in to provide guidance, but athletes themselves are taking the initiative to educate themselves about taxes, savings, and investments.

"I never thought I'd need an accountant at 19," one college quarterback joked. "But here we are."

High school athletes, meanwhile, are learning the value of saving for the future, with some even putting their NIL earnings toward college tuition or family expenses.

Priority #5: Giving Back

Many student-athletes are using their NIL success to make a difference in their communities. From donating a portion of their earnings to local charities to volunteering their time, athletes are finding ways to give back.

One high school volleyball player partnered with a local nonprofit to raise money for underprivileged kids. "It's not just about making money," she said. "It's about using my platform to help others."

For college athletes, giving back has also become a way to strengthen their personal brand and connect with fans. Whether it's hosting free sports clinics or supporting campus initiatives, these athletes are showing that NIL is about more than just personal gain - it's about making a positive impact.

The Humor: NIL Meets Student Life

Of course, the NIL era isn't all serious business. High school and college athletes are still finding time to have fun, whether it's sharing jokes about their sponsorships or poking fun at the challenges of balancing NIL with school and sports.

"One of my teammates got a deal with a local pizza place," a college swimmer shared. "Now every time he scores, we yell, 'That one's for the pepperoni!'"

High school athletes are also embracing the lighter side of NIL, with some jokingly asking their friends, "Do you think I could get a sponsorship for being the team's benchwarmer?"

These moments of humor remind everyone that, at the end of the day, student-athletes are still just kids trying to make the most of an extraordinary opportunity.

Looking Ahead: The Future of Student-athlete Priorities

As the NIL landscape continues to evolve, student-athletes are proving that they're up to the challenge. They're balancing school, sports, and business with grace and determination, all while staying focused on their dreams.

To the athletes out there: keep hustling, keep learning, and keep having fun. Whether you're signing endorsement deals, acing your chemistry test, or scoring the winning goal, you're paving the way for the future of sports.

Chapter 25
Sports Fans: Cheering, Debating, and Sliding into DMs

Sports fans have always been the lifeblood of athletics. They're the ones filling stadiums, arguing over rankings, and wearing face paint in freezing temperatures. The NIL era has added a new layer to the fan experience - one that's equal parts admiration, confusion, and, occasionally, jealousy.

High school and college athletes making big money from NIL deals have sparked some strong feelings among fans, ranging from enthusiastic support to heated debates. After all, it's not every day that your favorite point guard signs a six-figure sneaker deal or your high school's star quarterback lands a sponsorship with a national fast-food chain. So how are fans really feeling about all of this? Let's dive in.

The Supporters: "Get That Bag!"

A large and vocal group of fans is fully behind athletes making money from NIL deals. These are the folks who've long argued that student-athletes deserve to profit from their talents, especially when schools and organizations rake in billions from ticket sales, TV contracts, and merchandise.

For these fans, NIL is a long-overdue correction in the sports world. They cheer when a college volleyball player partners with an athletic wear company or when a high school sprinter gets an endorsement from a local shoe store. They see NIL as a win not just for athletes but also for fairness and equality in sports.

And let's be honest - some fans just love seeing athletes living their best lives. When a star running back posts a photo on Instagram with their new NIL-sponsored car, these fans are in the comments section typing, "You earned it, King!"

The Skeptics: "Is This Getting Out of Hand?"

On the flip side, some fans aren't so sure about this new NIL landscape. They worry it's creating a "pay-to-play" dynamic, where wealthier programs with more NIL opportunities have an unfair recruiting advantage. They also question whether teenagers and young adults can handle the pressures of fame, money, and expectations at such a young age.

These fans might say things like, "What happened to playing for the love of the game?" or "Do high school sophomores really need endorsement deals?" They're not necessarily against NIL - they just have concerns about how it's being managed and whether it's overshadowing the purity of sports.

And then there's the occasional grumble from fans that are a bit envious. ("Wait - this 17-year-old just got a $500,000 NIL deal, and I'm still paying off student loans?")

The Debaters: "Let's Argue About It!"

If there's one thing sports fans love more than watching games, it's debating about sports. The NIL era has provided plenty of fodder for heated discussions, both online and in person.

One popular topic is whether NIL deals are creating a divide within teams. "How do you think the backup kicker feels when the starting quarterback gets a car deal?" one fan might ask. Another might counter, "Well, the kicker can start posting trick shots on TikTok and land a deal of their own!"

Fans also debate the impact NIL has on college sports as a whole. Is it leveling the playing field or widening the gap between big and small programs? Is it empowering athletes or distracting them? And most importantly, is it time for fans to start NIL petitions for their favorite underappreciated players?

The Humor: Fans and NIL Shenanigans

Of course, the NIL era has also led to some hilarious moments for fans. Imagine scrolling through Twitter to see a high school wide receiver endorsing a local dentist's office with the tagline, "Catch passes, not cavities." Or a college swimmer promoting a brand of waterproof headphones with a cheesy (but catchy) slogan.

Fans have also taken to making playful suggestions for NIL deals. "Can we get the lineman a sponsorship with an all-you-can-eat buffet chain?" one fan might tweet. Or, "I need my favorite punter to partner with a coffee company because he keeps me awake during games."

And then there are the fans sliding into athletes' DMs - not to troll, but to pitch potential NIL collaborations. ("Hey, I own a landscaping business. Wanna partner up? Your nickname is 'The Lawn Mower' anyway!")

The Big Picture: Fan Loyalty Remains Strong

At the end of the day, one thing is clear: NIL hasn't diminished fans' love for sports or their favorite athletes. If anything, it's given fans a new way to connect with the players they admire.

Fans are now following athletes' social media accounts more closely than ever, not just to see game highlights but to cheer on their NIL successes. They're buying NIL-sponsored merchandise, supporting local businesses that partner with athletes, and celebrating the fact that young stars finally have a chance to profit from their hard work.

Yes, there are debates, concerns, and the occasional eyebrow raise. But for the most part, fans are adapting to the NIL era with the same passion and enthusiasm they bring to every game. After all, whether an athlete is scoring touchdowns, signing endorsement deals, or doing both at the same time, fans will always be there to cheer them on.

Looking Ahead: Fans in the NIL Era

As the NIL landscape continues to evolve, so will the fan experience. Perhaps we'll see more creative NIL collaborations, from e-sports athletes partnering with gaming companies to track stars endorsing fitness apps. Maybe fans themselves will get in on the action, crowdfunding NIL deals for their favorite players.

One thing's for sure: sports fans are as integral to the NIL era as the athletes themselves. Their cheers, debates, and even their jokes are part of what makes this new chapter in sports so exciting.

So, to the fans out there: keep cheering, keep debating, and keep supporting these young athletes. Because whether you're buying their NIL merch, liking their sponsored posts, or just shouting encouragement from the stands, you're helping shape the future of sports.

Chapter 26
The Future of the NIL Landscape: Big Dreams, Big Deals, and What's Next

The Growing NIL Economy: Bigger Deals, Broader Reach

If you think the NIL market is big now, just wait. Industry experts predict that the NIL economy will continue to grow at an astonishing rate, with more athletes signing deals and more companies jumping into the game.

NIL is no longer just about major college athletes landing six-figure contracts with national brands. High school athletes are getting in on the action, too, with local businesses, regional sponsors, and even niche brands eager to partner with young talent.

Some of the trends shaping the future of NIL include:

- **Non-Traditional Sports**: Athletes in sports like swimming, gymnastics, and e-sports are starting to see more NIL opportunities, proving that you don't have to play football or basketball to cash in.

- **Global Brands**: As social media continues to break down geographic barriers, international companies are looking to partner with American athletes, creating new opportunities for global exposure.

- **Micro-Influencers**: Not every athlete needs a massive following to succeed in the NIL era. Companies are increasingly turning to athletes with smaller, highly engaged audiences to promote their products.

As one marketing executive put it: "We used to sponsor just the quarterback. Now we're working with the entire offensive line - and the kicker."

The Role of Technology: NIL in the Digital Age

The future of NIL is closely tied to technology. From social media platforms to NIL-specific apps, technology is making it easier than ever for athletes to connect with sponsors, manage their deals, and grow their brands.

Some of the innovations shaping the NIL landscape include:

- **NIL Marketplaces**: Platforms that connect athletes with companies, streamlining the process of finding, negotiating, and signing deals.

- **AI Tools**: Artificial intelligence helps athletes analyze their social media performance, optimize their content, and even predict which brands might want to partner with them.

- **Blockchain and NFTs**: While still in their early stages, blockchain technology and NFTs (non-fungible tokens) are creating new ways for athletes to monetize their personal brands. Imagine owning a digital collectible of your favorite player's game-winning moment, it's closer to reality than you think.

And then there's the growing role of content creation. In the NIL era, athletes are becoming mini media companies, producing everything from behind - the - scenes vlogs to branded TikToks. The future of NIL will undoubtedly be shaped by the athletes who can master the art of storytelling.

The Regulatory Landscape: Finding the Right Balance

As NIL continues to grow, so does the need for clear, consistent regulations. The NIL landscape is still something of a patchwork, with different states, schools, and organizations enforcing their own rules.

But change is on the horizon. Policymakers are working toward creating a unified framework that ensures fairness, protects athletes, and provides clear guidelines for schools and companies.

Some of the key issues on the table include:

- **Age Limits**: Should there be restrictions on how young athletes can start signing NIL deals?

- **Tax Implications**: How can young athletes navigate the complex world of taxes and income reporting?

- **Equity and Inclusion**: How can NIL opportunities be distributed fairly, ensuring that athletes from all backgrounds and sports benefit?

While there's still work to be done, the future of NIL regulation is looking brighter, with a focus on protecting athletes and leveling the playing field.

The Impact on High School and College Sports

As NIL becomes more ingrained in the fabric of high school and college sports, it's reshaping the way athletes, schools, and fans approach the game.

For athletes, NIL is about more than just money - it's an opportunity to build life skills, gain financial independence, and set themselves up for success beyond sports. For schools, it's a chance to attract top talent, strengthen community ties, and showcase the value of their programs.

And for fans? NIL is creating new ways to connect with their favorite players, whether it's through social media, branded merchandise, or community events.

But with these opportunities come challenges. Schools are working hard to maintain team unity, prevent NIL from overshadowing academics, and ensure that athletes stay focused on their goals.

As one college coach said: "We tell our athletes: NIL is great, but it's not the endgame. It's just one part of your journey."

A Little Humor: NIL in 2030?

Of course, it wouldn't be NIL without a little humor. If the current trends continue, we can only imagine what the future might hold:

- A high school athlete signing a NIL deal with their local dentist for "the best smile in the league."

- A college swimmer partnering with a waterproof headphone company - because who wouldn't want to listen to music while doing laps?

- A kicker landing a deal with a sock brand that proudly advertises: "Perfect for kicking game-winning field goals."

The possibilities are endless, and the jokes practically write themselves.

Looking Ahead: NIL's Lasting Legacy

The future of NIL is bright, exciting, and full of potential. As the landscape continues to evolve, athletes, schools, and companies are finding new ways to collaborate, innovate, and grow.

But beyond the deals and dollars, the true legacy of NIL will be its impact on the lives of young athletes. By giving them the tools, resources, and opportunities to succeed, NIL is helping to shape the next generation of leaders - both on and off the field.

To the athletes, schools, and businesses leading the way: keep dreaming big, keep pushing boundaries, and keep finding ways to make NIL a force for good. Because the future of sports is here, and it's more exciting than ever.

Chapter 27
College Coaches MUST Adapt

"Adapt or Retire": How NIL is Forcing College Coaches to Evolve

The transformative effects of NIL deals on college athletics have reached a tipping point. For college coaches, the mantra has become clear: **"Adapt or Retire."** The pressure to navigate the complexities of NIL, transfer portals, and athlete branding has created a stark divide between coaches who embrace the new era and those who choose to step away. This chapter explores why adoption is essential for survival - and why some are opting to retire instead.

The NIL Revolution: A New Game for Coaches

The arrival of NIL in 2021 brought seismic changes to college sports, but now, its impact has permeated every level of the coaching profession. Coaches are no longer just strategists and recruiters; they are now expected to:

1. **Promote Athlete Branding**: Coaches must actively assist players in maximizing their NIL opportunities. This includes connecting athletes with sponsors, developing social media strategies, and ensuring compliance with NIL regulations.

2. **Manage NIL-Driven Recruitment**: A top recruit's decision may hinge on the NIL potential a program can offer. Coaches must now compete not just on the field but also in the marketplace, building partnerships with boosters, collectives,

and local businesses.

3. **Retain Talent Amid Transfer Portal Chaos**: The transfer portal, now more active than ever, has become a double-edged sword. Athletes dissatisfied with NIL opportunities at one school can quickly transfer to another. Coaches must work harder to retain their rosters, often requiring renegotiation of NIL deals.

Why Some Coaches Are Retiring

While some coaches have embraced the challenge, others are choosing to retire, citing the overwhelming demands of the NIL era. Here are the key reasons behind this exodus:

1. Increased Complexity and Stress

The traditional coaching job has morphed into a multi-faceted role that includes marketing, compliance, and public relations. Many veteran coaches feel unprepared or unwilling to take on these additional responsibilities. For example, iconic basketball coach Mike Krzyzewski, who retired in 2022, cited the rapid changes in college sports as one of the factors influencing his decision.

2. Shifting Power Dynamics

NIL has empowered athletes in unprecedented ways, giving them leverage over coaches in certain situations. Older coaches accustomed to a more hierarchical system sometimes struggle to adapt to this new athlete-first approach. For some, retirement becomes a more appealing option than adjusting to this paradigm shift.

3. Financial Security

Many high-profile coaches, particularly those with lucrative contracts and buyout clauses, have the financial luxury to step away. In the current climate, some coaches preemptively retire to avoid being ousted due to poor adaptation to NIL demands.

4. Ethical Concerns

Coaches who feel that NIL has commercialized college sports beyond recognition sometimes step down out of principle. They argue that the focus on money has diluted the spirit of amateur athletics and shifted priorities away from education and competition.

Coaches Who Are Adapting: The Blueprint for Success

For those who choose to stay, the path forward requires embracing innovation and adaptability. Here's how successful coaches are thriving in the NIL era:

1. Building NIL Support Systems

Top programs are creating NIL departments or partnerships with professional marketing agencies. Coaches who actively collaborate with these entities can offer athletes a competitive edge in securing deals.

- **Example**: Alabama football coach Nick Saban has embraced NIL by working closely with Crimson Tide collectives to secure opportunities for players, keeping the program competitive despite NIL-related challenges.

2. Leveraging the Transfer Portal

Rather than fearing the transfer portal, adaptive coaches use it to their advantage, targeting talented players who may have been overlooked or underutilized at other programs.

- **Example**: Deion Sanders at Colorado has turned the transfer portal into a weapon, rebuilding his roster with athletes seeking better NIL opportunities.

3. Adopting a Collaborative Leadership Style

Coaches who succeed in 2025 are those who embrace the athlete-centered approach demanded by the NIL era. They foster open communication, empowering athletes to take ownership of their brands while maintaining team cohesion.

The Future of Coaching in the NIL Era

The NIL-driven landscape has made coaching a more dynamic - and demanding - profession than ever before. While some retire rather than adapt to the new challenges, others see NIL as an opportunity to redefine the role of the coach in college athletics.

The Divide Will Grow

By 2030, the coaching profession may divide into two distinct categories:

- **Legacy Coaches**: Those who retire or transition out of the NCAA landscape, often citing NIL as a driving factor.

- **NIL Specialists**: A new generation of coaches, who see NIL as integral to their strategy, leveraging it to recruit, retain, and win.

The Path Forward

For coaches choosing to adapt, the key lies in embracing the entrepreneurial spirit of the NIL era. Those who can balance traditional coaching with the demands of the modern marketplace will not only survive but also thrive.

In the end, the choice is clear: **Adapt or step aside.**

Chapter 28
NIL Current Trends and Realities

1. The Professionalization of College Athletics

Today, NIL is no longer just about endorsement deals - it's a cornerstone of recruiting, branding, and career development. Universities now compete not only on facilities and scholarships but also on their NIL programs. Schools have established dedicated NIL departments, offering athletes resources like:

- **Brand - Building Workshops** to teach personal marketing.

- **Contract Negotiation Seminars** to avoid pitfalls.

- **Financial Literacy Courses** to help athletes manage their earnings.

Top-tier programs now boast NIL collectives - groups of boosters, alumni, and businesses working together to secure deals for athletes. These collectives have become critical recruiting tools, promising athletes' opportunities to earn significant income during their college careers.

---

2. High School Athletes and NIL

One of the biggest shifts since 2022 has been the extension of NIL rights to high school athletes. By 2023, more than 30 states passed laws allowing high schoolers to sign NIL deals. This trend exploded, with less than 10 states prohibiting teenage from endorsement deals and student athletes landing lucrative contracts even before stepping foot on a college campus.

For example, a high school basketball star recently signed a multi-million-dollar deal with a global sport drink Red Bull. Gymnasts and swimmers with viral social media followings have partnered with beauty and fashion companies. NIL has turned young athletes into household names, reshaping the recruiting process.

3. Social Media: The Golden Ticket

Social media remains the most powerful tool in the NIL era. Athletes with large followings on platforms like TikTok, Instagram, and YouTube are commanding deals worth tens of thousands - or even millions of dollars. It's not just about athletic performance anymore; personality and content creation now play a huge role in NIL success.

Take the example of a college quarterback who earns more from his comedy skits on TikTok than he does from football endorsements. Or the volleyball player-turned-lifestyle influencer who used NIL earnings to start her own fitness brand. Social media has democratized NIL, allowing athletes from all sports to thrive.

4. Educational Opportunities and Challenges

One of the most fascinating developments in the NIL era is its impact on education. Universities have embraced NIL as a teaching tool, offering courses in:

- **Entrepreneurship**: Many athletes are now CEOs of their own brands.

- **Digital Marketing**: Athletes learn how to grow and monetize their online presence.

- **Tax Law and Compliance**: Understanding taxes and contracts has become essential.

However, challenges remain. Some athletes struggle with balancing academics, sports, and the demands of NIL deals. Others face issues with predatory agents or poorly structured contracts. To address this, many schools now partner with legal and financial advisors to guide athletes through the complexities of NIL.

5. The NIL Economy

The financial impact of NIL is staggering. Experts estimate that the NIL industry generates over $4 billion annually. This includes:

- **Corporate Sponsorships**: From local businesses to multinational brands.

- **Merchandising**: Athletes selling personalized jerseys, apparel, and memorabilia.

- **Content Creation**: Revenue from YouTube ads, TikTok sponsorships, and more.

Interestingly, NIL has also boosted the NCAA's bottom line. Despite fears that NIL would destabilize college sports, increased attention and commercialization have only grown the audience for collegiate athletics.

The Impact of NIL: The Good, the Bad, and the Future

The Good

- **Empowerment**: Athletes now have control over their financial futures.

- **Opportunities for All**: NIL has leveled the playing field, benefiting athletes in lesser-known sports and women's athletics.

- **Life-Changing Earnings**: Many athletes use their NIL income to support their families, fund their education, or invest in businesses.

The Challenges

- **Equity**: Star athletes earn millions, while others struggle to secure deals.

- **Regulation**: Without a unified federal NIL law, state-by-state regulations create confusion.

- **Exploitation**: Some athletes fall victim to predatory deals or unscrupulous agents.

The Future

As we look ahead, NIL shows no signs of slowing down. Federal legislation is on the horizon, aiming to standardize NIL rules nationwide. Technology is also playing a role, with blockchain and

NFTs enabling athletes to monetize their likenesses in new ways. The future of NIL is as dynamic as the athletes it empowers.

Why NIL Matters More Than Ever

At its core, NIL is about fairness, empowerment, and opportunity. It's recognition that athletes are more than just players - they are entrepreneurs, influencers, and trailblazers. While the system isn't perfect, the progress made since 2022 is undeniable.

Looking back, NIL was never just about money. It was about giving athletes a voice, a platform, and a chance to take control of their destinies. And as we stand now, it's clear: NIL hasn't just changed the game, it's changed lives.

The game will never be the same, and that's exactly how it should be.

Chapter 29
Transfer Portal: When Opportunity Knocks

In the world of high school and college sports, two words have become as game-changing as a buzzer-beater: **Transfer Portal**. Combine it with NIL (Name, Image, and Likeness), and you've got a recipe for one of the biggest shifts in how young athletes approach their careers. The transfer portal has become more than a tool - it's a lifeline, a business opportunity, and for some, a golden ticket to better exposure and bigger paydays.

But let's not sugarcoat it: the transfer portal is also a whirlwind. For athletes, coaches, and fans, it can feel like the Wild West. Teams are constantly in flux, loyalty is being redefined, and the stakes have never been higher. Add NIL deals into the mix, and you've got a dynamic that's as thrilling as it is unpredictable.

What Is the Transfer Portal?

For those who may not be NCAA insiders, the transfer portal is essentially a digital database where college athletes can enter their names to signal they're considering transferring schools. Think of it as LinkedIn for student-athletes, but with fewer boring office selfies and more highlight reels.

Before the portal, athletes who wanted to transfer often had to sit out a year, a rule that deterred many. But in recent years, those restrictions have been relaxed, and now the portal is booming. Add in NIL, and the portal isn't just about finding a better fit on the field - it's about finding better financial opportunities.

How NIL and the Portal Work Together

Here's the real kicker: the transfer portal isn't just about playing time anymore. In the NIL era, it's more about brand-building, marketability, and securing the best deals.

Imagine this: a star running back at a smaller Division I school is excelling on the field, but his NIL opportunities are limited because the school lacks major media exposure. Enter the transfer portal. By transferring to a powerhouse program with a larger fan base and national TV appearances, that same athlete can dramatically increase his market value. Suddenly, the local car dealership deal becomes a national sports drink endorsement.

It's not just hypothetical - it's happening. In 2025, we've seen athletes leverage the portal to maximize their NIL potential. Some have even negotiated NIL deals as part of their recruitment process, creating a new dynamic where schools, boosters, and sponsors are working together to land top talent.

High School Athletes and the Portal

The transfer portal isn't just shaking up college sports; it's trickling down to high school athletes, too. With NIL now extending to certain high school athletes in states that allow it, transferring to a different high school for better exposure is becoming common. It's no longer just about playing for the hometown team; it's about positioning yourself for bigger opportunities down the line.

For example, a high school basketball star might transfer to a prep academy with a national schedule to increase their visibility - and their NIL value. And while this can lead to incredible opportunities, it also raises tough questions about loyalty, community, and the balance between chasing dreams and staying grounded.

The Good, the Bad, and the Chaotic

Let's break it down:

- **The Good**: The transfer portal gives athletes agency. If they're stuck in a situation where their skills aren't being utilized or they're not getting the exposure they need, the portal offers a fresh start. For many, it's a game-changer that can lead to better opportunities both on and off the field.

- **The Bad**: The portal isn't always a guaranteed path to success. Some athletes enter without a clear plan, only to find themselves without a scholarship or a team. And while NIL deals can sweeten the pot, they can also add pressure. Imagine being 19 years old and having to weigh the financial implications of transferring - it's not easy.

- **The Chaotic**: Let's not forget the whirlwind this creates for coaches and programs. Building a cohesive team is harder than ever when rosters are constantly changing. And for fans? It can be tough to keep track of who's playing where.

A Balancing Act

At its core, the relationship between NIL and the transfer portal is about balance. For athletes, it's about weighing short-term gains against long-term goals. For schools, it's about finding ways to stay competitive without losing sight of the bigger picture. And for everyone else, it's about adapting to a new era where change is the only constant.

The Future of NIL and the Portal

Looking ahead, it's clear that NIL and the transfer portal are here to stay. But as the system evolves, so will the rules, strategies, and expectations. We may see more structured guidelines around NIL recruitment, or perhaps new tools to help athletes make informed decisions.

One thing is certain: the transfer portal, like NIL, is all about opportunity. For athletes, it's a chance to take control of their futures. For schools and brands, it's a chance to rethink how they approach talent and partnerships. And for the rest of us, it's a chance to witness the evolution of sports in real time.

Parting Words

The transfer portal and NIL have created a fascinating, fast-moving world where athletes are no longer just players, they're decision-makers, entrepreneurs, and, sometimes, risk-takers. It's not always smooth sailing, but for those who navigate it wisely, the rewards can be life changing.

So here's to the athletes making bold moves, the parents and coaches supporting them, and the fans cheering from the sidelines. The game has changed, and the transfer portal is proof that when opportunity knocks, the best players don't just answer the door - they sprint through it. And who knows? The next big NIL star might already be scrolling through the portal, looking for their next big break.

Chapter 30
It's Not WHAT You Know, It's WHO You Know for NIL Deals

One thing is clear in the world of NIL: talent gets you noticed, but connections close the deal. High school and college athletes are building their brands, showcasing their skills, and dreaming of those lucrative sponsorships with major companies. But here's the kicker - most families quickly realize they don't have the direct line to big-name brands like Nike, Gatorade, or Beats by Dre.

The truth? In the NIL game, personal and business connections are often the secret sauce to success. It's not just about how many points you score or how many followers you have on Instagram. It's about knowing someone who knows someone who can get you in the door. And for most athletes and their families, that means turning to third parties - agents, marketing professionals, and NIL specialists - to bridge the gap.

Let's dive into why these connections matter, how to build them, and what athletes and families need to know to navigate this relationship-driven world of NIL deals.

The Problem: No Direct Line to Brands

For the average high school or college athlete, getting in touch with major brands feels like trying to text your celebrity crush impossible. These companies are flooded with requests, and unless you're already a household name, it's unlikely they'll come knocking on your door.

Parents, too, often find themselves in over their heads. They might have the best intentions, but unless they happen to work in marketing or have connections in the corporate world, they're just as lost as their kids. And the general public? Forget about it. Most people wouldn't even know where to start.

So, how do athletes go from dreaming about an endorsement deal to actually signing one? That's where third parties come in.

The Role of Third Parties

In the NIL era, third parties are the behind-the-scenes MVPs. These are the managers, marketing reps, and NIL consultants who have one crucial asset: relationships. They know the decision-makers at brands, they understand what companies are looking for, and they can pitch athletes in a way that gets results.

Here's how they make the magic happen:

1. **Leveraging Existing Relationships**: Third parties often have long - standing connections with brands. They know who to call, how to craft a compelling pitch, and what kind of athletes each company is interested in.

2. **Identifying the Right Fit**: Not every athlete is a match for every brand. Third parties help athletes find companies that align with their image and values - whether it's a sneaker deal for a basketball player or a protein bar endorsement for a runner.

3. **Negotiating Deals**: Once a brand shows interest, third parties handle the negotiations. They ensure athletes get fair terms, competitive pay, and opportunities that make sense for their

careers.

4. **Managing the Relationship**: The work doesn't stop once the deal is signed. Third parties often help athletes fulfill their obligations, like attending events or posting on social media, while keeping the brand happy.

Why Connections Matter

Here's the reality: NIL deals aren't just about talent. They're about visibility. Brands want athletes who can help them reach new audiences, and third parties help athletes get on those brands' radar.

Take this real-life example: A college volleyball player with a modest social media following landed a deal with a national sports apparel brand. How? Her NIL consultant had a personal relationship with the brand's marketing director and was able to pitch her as a perfect fit for a new campaign targeting young women in sports. Without that connection, the deal might never have happened.

Building Your Team

So, how do families find the right third party to help their athlete succeed in the NIL world? Here are some tips:

1. **Look for Transparency**: A good third party will be upfront about their connections, their strategy, and what they can realistically deliver. If someone promises the moon, proceed with caution.

2. **Do Your Research**: Not all managers, consultants and agents are created equal. Look for professionals with a proven track record in NIL and strong connections in the industry.

3. **Ask for Recommendations**: Other athletes and families can be a great resource. Don't be afraid to ask who they're working with and whether they'd recommend them.

4. **Understand the Costs**: Third parties don't work for free. Some take a percentage of the athlete's NIL earnings, while others charge flat fees. Make sure you understand the terms before signing any agreements.

The Humor in the Hustle

Let's take a moment to appreciate the absurdity of the NIL process. Imagine a parent cold-calling Nike's headquarters:

"Hi, my son just scored three touchdowns last Friday, and we think he'd be a great fit for your next campaign!"

The odds of that working? Slim to none. But hey, at least they tried.

One athlete recently joked on social media: "My mom said she emailed Gatorade about sponsoring me, but all she got back was an automated response. Guess it's time to hire an agent."

The truth is, the NIL world is complex, and while personal hustle is admirable, having a professional team with the right connections makes all the difference.

The Bigger Picture

NIL isn't just about making money - it's about building a career. The right connections can open doors that lead to long-term partnerships, greater visibility, and opportunities beyond sports.

But it's also important to remember that not every athlete needs a million-dollar deal to succeed. Sometimes, smaller, local endorsements can be just as impactful, especially for athletes who are new to NIL.

And for families, the key is finding balance. Yes, connections matter, but so do values, integrity, and staying true to what makes the athlete unique.

Closing Thoughts

In the NIL era, connections are king. Whether it's a third-party agent with ties to major brands or a local business owner who wants to support their community, the people you know can make or break an athlete's NIL journey.

For athletes and families, the message is clear: don't be afraid to ask for help, invest in the right team, and lean into the power of relationships. And remember, every deal starts with a conversation - so make sure you're talking to the right people.

As the saying goes, it's not what you know, it's who you know. And in NIL, the right "who" can turn dreams into dollars faster than a sprinter in the 100-meter dash.

So, let's raise a Gatorade (or whatever brand you're endorsing) to the agents, consultants, and connectors making it all happen - and to the athletes who are smart enough to play the game both on and off the field. Cheers to that!

Chapter 31
Revenue-Sharing: The Cost of Playing the NIL Game and the New Reality

While the idea of sharing revenue with student-athletes sounds straightforward, the reality is anything but. For schools, the costs associated with these models are skyrocketing, and athletic departments are learning to navigate a landscape where the line between amateur and professional sports has never been blurrier.

The Revenue-Sharing Model: How It Works

In 2025, the revenue-sharing model became a cornerstone of the NIL era at many schools, especially those in Power Five conferences where sports like football and basketball generate millions (sometimes billions) in revenue. Here's how it typically works:

1. **Revenue Pooling**

    A percentage of the revenue generated by a school's athletic department - primarily from media rights, ticket sales, merchandise, and sponsorships set aside for student-athletes.

2. **Distribution**

    The money is then distributed among athletes, either equally across all sports or weighted based on factors like the revenue generated by specific programs. For example, a football quarterback at a major Division I school might receive a larger share than a swimmer at the same school.

3. **Compliance and Oversight**

   Schools must ensure that revenue-sharing payments comply with NCAA rules, state laws, and federal tax requirements. Spoiler: this is as fun as it sounds.

The Costs of Revenue Sharing

For schools with major sports programs, revenue sharing represents a significant financial commitment:

1. **Power Five Conference Schools**

   In 2025, the average Power Five school generates upwards of $150 million annually in athletic revenue. With revenue-sharing agreements typically allocating 10-15% of that revenue to athletes, schools are paying out anywhere from $15 to $22 million per year.

2. **Mid-Major Schools**
   For schools outside the Power Five, revenue-sharing costs are lower in absolute terms but often represent a higher percentage of their overall athletic budgets. A mid-major school generating $30 million in revenue might still be on the hook for $3 to $5 million in athlete payments - a significant strain on their resources.

3. **Non-Revenue Sports**
   While football and basketball drive the bulk of revenue, schools are also grappling with how to support athletes in non-revenue sports. Many programs rely on subsidies from

the revenue generators, creating tension as schools try to balance fairness with financial reality.

Where Is the Money Coming From?

To fund revenue-sharing agreements, schools are turning to a mix of strategies:

1. **Increased Media Rights Deals**

    The explosion of streaming platforms and media rights negotiations has brought in record-breaking revenue for major conferences. Schools are banking on these deals to offset the costs of revenue sharing.

2. **Boosters and Donors**

    Schools are leaning heavily on their alumni networks and booster clubs to fill the gaps. One athletic director joked, "If I had a dollar for every time I asked a donor for another dollar, I wouldn't need to ask anymore."

3. **Ticket Price Increases**

    Fans are starting to feel the impact of revenue sharing in their wallets, as schools raise ticket prices to keep up with expenses. One fan quipped, "I'm happy to support the athletes, but at these prices, I'm expecting a signed jersey with my nachos."

4. **Cutbacks in Other Areas**
    Some schools are making tough choices, cutting back on

facility upgrades, administrative staff, or even non-revenue sports programs to balance the books.

The Challenges Schools Face

The costs of revenue sharing are just one piece of the puzzle. Schools are also grappling with a host of challenges that make the NIL era especially tricky to navigate:

1. **Equity and Fairness**

    Deciding how to distribute revenue among athletes is a minefield. Should athletes in revenue-generating sports get a larger share? What about walk-ons or athletes in non-revenue sports? Schools are trying to strike a balance, but there's no one-size-fits-all answer.

2. **Tax Implications**

    Revenue-sharing payments are considered taxable income, which means schools need to educate athletes on tax responsibilities. One AD quipped, "We've gone from teaching zone defense to teaching W-2s."

3. **Public Perception**

    Not everyone is thrilled about revenue sharing. Critics argue that it blurs the line between college and professional sports, while some fans worry that the focus on money is overshadowing the spirit of amateur athletics.

4. **Sustainability**

   The big question looming over revenue sharing is whether it's sustainable in the long term. For schools without deep pockets, the financial strain is real, and some are questioning whether they can keep up.

Looking Ahead

So, what's next for schools navigating the costs of revenue sharing? The future is still taking shape, but a few trends are emerging:

1. **Innovation in Fundraising**

   Schools are getting creative, launching new fundraising campaigns, partnering with local businesses, and even exploring NIL collectives to support athletes and offset costs.

2. **Collaboration Across Conferences**

   Conferences are working together to develop standardized revenue-sharing models, creating consistency and reducing the administrative burden on individual schools.

3. **Evolving the Model**

   As the NIL era matures, schools may refine their revenue-sharing agreements, exploring new ways to balance athlete compensation with long-term financial sustainability.

A Message to Schools

To the schools navigating the costs of revenue sharing: we see you. You're trying to do right by your athletes, your fans, and your bottom line, and it's no easy task. But remember this: the NIL era is about more than dollars and cents. It's about creating opportunities and empowering the next generation of leaders.

So, keep crunching the numbers, keep advocating for your programs, and don't forget to take a moment to laugh at the ridiculousness of it all. Because in this world of *No Immediate Loyalty,* one thing is certain: the game is always changing, but the mission remains the same.

Chapter 32
Smaller D1 Schools: The Revenue Squeeze

For smaller Division I schools without football programs, the NIL-driven revenue-sharing model presents a unique set of challenges. Unlike their Power Five peers, these schools don't have the financial windfall of multi-million-dollar TV deals or packed stadiums on Saturdays. Instead, they rely on smaller revenue streams - often centered around basketball, Olympic sports, or donor contributions to fund their athletic programs.

Financial Reality

The revenue-sharing model has been a boon for student-athletes, but for smaller Division I schools, it's a financial strain. Here's why:

1. **Limited Revenue Streams**

    Without football, a major moneymaker for larger school - these institutions rely heavily on basketball and a mix of Olympic sports for revenue. But even basketball programs at smaller schools don't generate the kind of revenue seen in Power Five conferences.

For example, the average mid-major basketball program might generate $2 to $5 million annually, compared to the tens of millions pulled in by schools like Duke or Kentucky. When you're working with smaller budgets, carving out a chunk for revenue-sharing becomes a daunting task.

2. **Donor and Booster Fatigue**

   Smaller schools often lean heavily on donors and boosters to fund their athletic programs. However, with the added demands of revenue-sharing, these donors are being asked to contribute more than ever. As one athletic director put it, "You can only ask someone to buy so many raffle tickets before they start screening your calls."

3. **The Cost of Staying Competitive**

   Revenue-sharing isn't just about cutting checks - it's also about ensuring your facilities, coaching staff, and overall program remain attractive to recruits. For smaller schools, every dollar spent on revenue sharing is a dollar that can't be invested elsewhere, creating a delicate balancing act.

The Recruiting Challenge

In the NIL era, recruits are increasingly savvy about the financial opportunities available to them. For smaller Division I schools, this creates a recruiting challenge: how do you attract top talent when you can't offer the same revenue-sharing payouts or NIL opportunities as larger programs?

Here are obstacles smaller schools face:

1. **The Perception Gap**

   Recruits may view smaller schools as less appealing simply because they don't have the same financial resources as their Power Five counterparts. Convincing athletes that they can still thrive at a smaller program requires a strong pitch -

and a little creativity.

2. **Competing with NIL Collectives**

   Power Five schools often have well-funded NIL collectives that pool resources from donors and businesses to support athletes. Smaller schools, without the same network of wealthy alumni or local corporate sponsors, struggle to compete.

3. **Retention Risks**

   Even if a smaller school lands a talented recruit, keeping them is another story. The transfer portal has made it easier than ever for athletes to jump to bigger programs with more lucrative opportunities, leaving smaller schools in a constant cycle of rebuilding.

How Smaller Schools Can Stay Competitive

Despite the challenges, smaller Division I schools are finding ways to adapt and thrive in the NIL and revenue-sharing era. Here are some strategies they're using to stay competitive:

1. Focus on the Athlete Experience

Smaller schools have always excelled at creating tight-knit, supportive environments for their athletes. By emphasizing personal development, academic success, and individualized attention, these schools can offer recruits something that bigger programs often can't: a sense of community.

For example, schools can highlight smaller class sizes, better access to professors, and opportunities for leadership roles on campus. As one coach put it, "We may not have a 100,000-seat stadium, but we know every athlete's name - and their favorite post-game meal."

2. Leverage Specialized NIL Opportunities

While smaller schools may not have the same NIL infrastructures as Power Five programs, they can still create opportunities for their athletes. This might include partnerships with local businesses, alumni-owned companies, or regional sponsors who value the connection to the community.

For instance, a basketball star at a smaller school could partner with a local coffee shop or fitness studio, building a personal brand that resonates with the fan base.

3. Invest in Key Sports

Without football, smaller schools often rely on one or two marquee programs - such as basketball or volleyball - to drive their athletic success. By focusing resources on these sports, schools can create a "flagship program" that attracts recruits, generates revenue, and raises the profile of the entire athletic department.

Take Gonzaga, for example. The school doesn't have a football program, but its powerhouse basketball team has become a national brand, attracting top recruits and generating significant revenue.

However, smaller schools with no football program and no national basketball program, like *Pepperdine University in Malibu, California*, must decide to invest in the basketball program to get to the next level and national exposure. It's not just about paying the athletes, but building a new basketball arena sports complex like the one

Pepperdine is building to open in 2026 season, will attract talented athletes.

4. Collaborate with Conferences

Smaller schools are increasingly working together within their conferences to pool resources and create collective NIL opportunities. For example, a conference-wide NIL initiative could allow athletes at all member schools to benefit from shared sponsorships, creating a more level playing field.

5. Emphasize Academic and Career Development

For athletes who may not go pro, the promise of a strong academic foundation and career development opportunities can be a major selling point. Smaller schools can partner with local businesses to offer internships, career training, and mentorship programs, positioning themselves as a launch pad for life beyond sports.

6. Innovative Fundraising

Smaller schools are getting creative with fundraising, launching campaigns that appeal directly to fans and alumni. For example, schools might create crowdfunding campaigns to support specific sports or initiatives, allowing supporters to feel directly connected to the athletes they're helping.

7. Fundraising Distribution and Hiring Great Coaching Staff That Develops the Players

The smaller schools are going to invest in developing kids in high school, junior college or Academies. These schools will pay them a very small amount of money for their freshman and sophomore years. If the coaching staff does a great job developing the talent, the schools will retain these kids by giving them the big pay their final two years.

My System That Will Work for Smaller D1 Schools:

1. Recruit players who want to go your college

2. Free Scholarship and small pay first year or two

3. Develop the kids with great coaching

4. Retain them by paying them well once they break out

The smaller schools are getting creative with fundraising, launching campaigns that appeal directly to fans and alumni. For example, schools might create crowdfunding campaigns to support specific sports or initiatives, allowing supporters to feel directly connected to the athletes they're helping.

A Message to Smaller Schools

To the smaller Division I schools navigating the revenue-sharing era: you're the underdogs, the scrappy fighters, the ones who prove that heart and hustle can compete with big budgets and bright lights.

Yes, the challenges are real. But so are the opportunities. By focusing on what makes your programs unique - whether it's community, academics, or the athlete experience - you can continue to attract recruits, build successful teams, and thrive in this new landscape.

And if all else fails, remember in this world of *No Immediate Loyalty*, the underdogs often have the best stories. So, keep writing your chapter - and don't forget to enjoy the ride. Now, back to work. The next Gonzaga or Butler is out there, and it might just be you.

Chapter 33
Ivy League vs. NIL: First-Class Education, No Cash on Delivery

In the high-stakes, big-money world of the NIL era, where student-athletes are securing six-figure endorsement deals and schools are cutting checks through revenue-sharing models, the Ivy League stands apart like a tweed-clad professor at a fraternity party.

The Ivy League has long been an island in the sea of college athletics, priding itself on academic rigor, amateurism, and tradition. And in 2025, as many major programs are paying athletes to compete, the Ivies are sticking to their philosophy: no athletic scholarships, no direct pay to athletes, and no revenue-sharing checks. Instead, they're offering something else - a first-class education, unparalleled networking opportunities, and a promise that their athletes will leave campus better prepared for life beyond the game.

So how are the Ivy League schools navigating the NIL era, when the rest of the collegiate sports world is putting dollar signs front and center? And can they stay competitive without paying athletes? Let's dive in.

The Ivy League Stance on NIL

The Ivy League's approach to NIL can be summed up in one word: *consistent.*

1. **No Athletic Scholarships**

   Unlike most Division I schools, Ivy League institutions have never offered athletic scholarships. Instead, they provide need-based financial aid packages that are often as generous - or more so - than traditional scholarships.

2. **No Revenue-Sharing**

   While Power Five schools are setting aside millions in revenue-sharing agreements; the Ivy League has opted out of this trend entirely. Their reasoning? Ivy League athletics are meant to complement academics, not overshadow them.

3. **Embracing NIL - With Limits**

   Ivy League athletes are allowed to profit from NIL opportunities, just like their counterparts at other schools. However, the league isn't facilitating NIL deals or creating NIL collectives. Athletes are largely left to pursue those opportunities on their own, often with the help of outside advisors or family members.

The Cost Equation: Ivy League vs. Revenue-Sharing

For many schools, the NIL era has brought massive financial pressures. Revenue-sharing agreements, increased NIL-related staffing, and skyrocketing compliance costs are straining athletic budgets. But for the Ivy League, the financial equation looks very different.

1. **No Direct Payments to Athletes**

   By not participating in revenue-sharing models, Ivy League schools have avoided the multi-million-dollar costs that are now standard at Power Five programs.

2. **Focus on Financial Aid**

   Instead of paying athletes directly; Ivy League schools use their robust endowments to fund need-based financial aid. For many athletes, this means attending an Ivy League school can still be affordable-without the need for athletic scholarships or NIL payouts.

3. **Maintaining Tradition**

   By sticking to their amateurism roots, Ivy League schools are avoiding the financial arms race that's consuming many other athletic departments. As one Ivy League athletic director put it, "We're not trying to outspend anyone. We're trying to out-educate everyone."

Why Athletes Still Choose the Ivy League

You might be wondering: in a world where athletes can cash in on NIL opportunities and earn revenue - sharing payouts, why would anyone choose an Ivy League school? The answer lies in what the Ivies offer that money can't buy.

1. **A World-Class Education**

   An Ivy League degree is still one of the most coveted credentials in the world. For many athletes, the long-term value of that education far outweighs the short-term financial benefits of NIL or revenue sharing.

2. **Networking Opportunities**

   Ivy League schools are famous for their alumni networks, which can open doors to careers in business, law, medicine, and more. As one Ivy League athlete put it, "I can't cash a check from my football career, but I can call a CEO who went to my school."

3. **The Prestige Factor**

   There's a certain prestige that comes with being both a student and an athlete at an Ivy League school. For some recruits, that's worth more than any endorsement deal.

4. **NIL Opportunities - Just Different Ones**

   While Ivy League athletes may not have the same flashy NIL opportunities as their Power Five counterparts, they're still finding ways to capitalize on their name, image, and likeness. For example, a Harvard rower might partner with a luxury watch brand, or a Princeton basketball player might write a book about balancing academics and athletics.

The Challenges of Staying Competitive

Of course, the Ivy League's approach to NIL isn't without its challenges.

1. **Recruiting Against Revenue-Sharing Schools**

   Convincing a recruit to choose an Ivy League school over a

program offering a six-figure revenue-sharing payout is no small feat. Coaches are leaning heavily on the promise of a world-class education and the long-term benefits of an Ivy League experience.

2. **The Transfer Portal**

    The transfer portal has made it easier than ever for athletes to leave one school for another. Ivy League programs, which can't offer financial incentives to stay, are at risk of losing athletes to schools with deeper pockets.

3. **Balancing Tradition and Modernity**

    As college sports continue to evolve, the Ivy League faces pressure to adapt without compromising its core values. Walking that line is no easy task.

The Humor in the Ivy League Approach

If there's one thing Ivy League schools have, it's a sense of humor about their unique place in the NIL landscape.

One Ivy League coach joked, "We may not have the biggest stadiums, but we do have the biggest libraries."

Another quipped, "Our recruiting pitch is simple: We can't pay you now, but in 20 years, you'll be running the company that sponsors the other schools' athletes."

And then there's the athlete who, when asked why they chose an Ivy League school, said, "Because I wanted to be a student-athlete, not an athlete-student."

Looking Ahead

So, what's next for the Ivy League in the NIL era? While they're unlikely to embrace revenue-sharing or athletic scholarships anytime soon, the Ivies are finding ways to stay relevant:

1. **Enhanced Athlete Support**

   Expect Ivy League schools to invest more in resources to help athletes navigate the NIL landscape, such as career counseling, financial literacy programs, and connections to alumni in the sports and business worlds.

2. **Leveraging Alumni Networks**

   The Ivy League's alumni networks are a goldmine for athletes seeking post-graduation opportunities. Schools will continue to highlight this advantage in recruiting pitches.

3. **Doubling Down on Academics**

   By emphasizing the long-term value of an Ivy League education, these schools are carving out a niche that sets them apart from revenue - sharing programs.

A Message to Ivy League Athletes

To the athletes choosing the Ivy League over big-money programs: you're playing the long game. You're betting on yourself, your education, and your future - and that's a winning strategy.

Yes, you might miss out on some of the short - term flash and cash of the NIL era. But remember in this world of ***No Immediate Loyalty***, the Ivy League is offering something rare - a foundation that will last a lifetime.

And hey, when you're running the Fortune 500 Company that sponsors the next generation of athletes, be sure to tell them where you got your start.

Chapter 34
General Managers Hired at High Schools and Colleges: The New MVPs

In the ever-evolving NIL era, the phrase "stick to sports" has truly gone out the window. Schools are no longer just running athletic programs; they're essentially running multi-million-dollar businesses. And with revenue-sharing models, NIL deals, compliance nightmares, and the transfer portal all piling on, athletic departments are finding themselves in desperate need of someone who can bring order to chaos. Enter the newest MVP of college sports: the *General Manager.*

Yes, you read that right. High schools and colleges across the country are hiring General Managers to oversee their athletic departments. These GMs are part executive, part strategist, part compliance officer, and part counselor. Their job? To make sure everything - from athlete payments to NIL deals to team rosters - runs like a well-oiled machine. Or at least doesn't spontaneously combust.

Mater Dei High School, a California private school nationally known for its strong sports programs, has inked a 10-year multimedia rights deal with the media and marketing company Playfly Sports. It's believed to be the first time a high school has signed a third-party multimedia rights deal. The landmark agreement is valued in the "high seven-figure" range, according to someone familiar with the deal. Mater Dei, located in Santa Ana, Calif., aims to leverage Playfly's resources to drive revenue opportunities across sponsorship, merchandise and digital media. The Catholic college preparatory school is hoping the addition of new national corporate partners and an enhanced game day experience at Santa Ana Stadium will ease pressure in its ongoing fundraising efforts.

The Cost of NIL and Revenue-Sharing

Before we get to the General Managers, let's talk about why they're so desperately needed.

In 2025, the financial demands of the NIL era are staggering - especially for schools that have embraced revenue-sharing models. Here's the reality:

1. **College Costs**

   For major Division I programs, revenue sharing has added tens of millions of dollars to their annual budgets. Schools in Power Five conferences are allocating anywhere from 10% to 15% of their athletic revenue to student-athletes, which can amount to $15 million or more per year.

2. **High School Costs**

   While not every state allows high school athletes to profit from NIL deals, those that do are seeing new pressures on athletic budgets. Schools are scrambling to provide the infrastructure - compliance officers, financial education, and NIL resources - needed to support their athletes.

3. **Administrative Burden**

   On top of the financial strain, schools are drowning in paperwork. From tracking NIL deals to managing athlete payments to ensuring compliance with state and federal laws, the administrative workload has grown exponentially.

The Rise of the General Manager

Faced with these challenges, schools are turning to a solution borrowed straight from the professional sports playbook: hiring General Managers.

What Does a GM Do?

Unlike athletic directors, who oversee the big-picture goals of an athletic department, GMs are laser-focused on operations. Their responsibilities include:

- **Overseeing Revenue Sharing**: Managing the distribution of payments to student-athletes and ensuring the process is fair, transparent, and compliant with all regulations.

- **NIL Deal Coordination**: Helping athletes navigate the NIL landscape by connecting them with opportunities, vetting contracts, and liaising with businesses and sponsors.

- **Managing the Transfer Portal**: Tracking roster changes, recruiting transfers, and ensuring teams remain competitive in a world where athletes can change schools with the swipe of an app.

- **Budget Oversight**: Balancing the books, identifying new revenue streams, and finding creative ways to fund athletic programs without cutting corners (or sports).

- **Compliance and Education**: Ensuring that athletes, coaches, and staff understand the rules around NIL and revenue sharing - and don't accidentally tank a program with a tweet.

Who's Hiring GMs?

- **Power Five Schools**: GMs are quickly becoming standard at major programs, where the stakes (and budgets) are highest.

- **Mid-Major and Small Colleges**: Even smaller schools are getting in on the trend, recognizing that a skilled GM can help them stay competitive in a crowded market.

- **High Schools**: While less common, some high schools in NIL-friendly states are hiring GMs or similar roles to manage NIL opportunities for their athletes.

Why GMs Are a Game-Changer

General Managers are reshaping the way high schools and colleges approach athletics. Here's why they're making such an impact:

1. **Efficiency**

   With GMs handling the operational side of things, athletic directors can focus on strategy, fundraising, and big-picture goals. This division of labor has been a game-changer for many schools.

2. **Professionalism**

   In the NIL era, college and even high school sports are starting to resemble professional leagues. GMs bring a level of expertise and professionalism that helps schools compete in this new environment.

3. **Athlete Support**

   By coordinating NIL deals, managing payments, and providing education, GMs ensure that athletes are supported both on and off the field. This not only helps athletes succeed but also makes programs more attractive to recruits.

The Challenges of Hiring GMs

Of course, hiring a GM isn't a magic bullet. Schools face several challenges as they embrace this new role:

1. **Cost**

   Adding a GM to the payroll isn't cheap, especially for smaller schools and high schools with limited budgets. Some institutions are struggling to justify the expense, even as they recognize the need.

2. **Finding the Right Fit**

   A good GM needs to be part business strategist, part compliance expert, and part people person. Finding someone with the right mix of skills isn't easy - and the competition for top talent is fierce.

3. **Adjusting to the New Normal**

   For some schools, the idea of hiring a GM feels more "pro sports" than "college athletics." Adjusting to this new reality requires a cultural shift, not just a budget line item.

The Humor in the Hustle

If there's one thing we've learned in the NIL era, it's that you have to laugh to keep from crying.

One athletic director joked, "I walked into my GM's office the other day, and they were explaining TikTok algorithms to a golfer. I don't know what's more impressive - the golfer's NIL deal or the fact that we have a GM who speaks fluent Gen Z."

Another AD shared a story about a GM who negotiated a group NIL deal for an entire volleyball team. "They called it the 'Serve and Earn' campaign. I told them they missed an opportunity to call it 'Set for Life.'"

And then there's the high school principal who, when asked why they hired a GM, said, "Because I already have 500 students to manage. I don't have time to explain to a 16-year-old why they can't endorse a vape shop."

Looking Ahead

As the NIL era continues to evolve, the role of General Manager is likely to become even more essential. Schools that invest in this position today are setting themselves up for success in the future, while those that resist may find themselves falling behind.

The question isn't whether GMs are here to stay; it's how schools will adapt to make the most of them. For some, that might mean hiring a full-time GM. For others, it might mean sharing resources or partnering with outside firms. Either way, the message is clear: the game has changed, and schools need to change with it.

A Message to GMs

To the General Managers out there: you're the unsung heroes of the NIL era. You're juggling contracts, budgets, and compliance with the grace of a point guard and the patience of a monk. Keep doing what you're doing - and don't forget to take a moment to laugh at the absurdity of it all.

Because in this world of *No Immediate Loyalty*, where athletes transfer, deals change, and the rules are rewritten daily, one thing is certain: the GM is the glue holding it all together.

Now, back to the spreadsheets. There's a transfer portal to navigate, a sponsorship deal to vet, and a basketball coach who still doesn't understand TikTok. You've got this.

Chapter 35
Challenges Facing the NCAA

The NIL era has created a host of challenges for the NCAA, many of which are still unresolved.

1. Patchwork Policies

With no federal NIL law in place, schools and athletes operate under a confusing mix of state laws and institutional policies. Some states allow high school athletes to profit from NIL, while others don't. Some schools have NIL collectives that rival professional team payrolls, while others are struggling to keep up.

The result? A competitive landscape that's anything but level. One NCAA official joked, "Trying to enforce fairness in NIL is like trying to referee a game where everyone's playing by different rules - and one team brought their own ball."

2. Athlete Employment Status

One of the biggest debates is whether college athletes should be classified as employees. Several lawsuits and unionization efforts are challenging the NCAA's long-standing stance that athletes are amateurs. If courts or Congress rule that athletes are employees, it could fundamentally change the NCAA's role - and its finances.

3. Competitive Balance

The NCAA's mission to promote competitive balance feels increasingly like a distant dream. NIL has created a world where the richest schools (and their collectives) can offer the most lucrative opportunities, leaving smaller programs to fight for scraps. It's hard to enforce parity when one school's quarterback has a seven-figure NIL deal, and another school's entire roster is sharing a sponsorship from a local diner.

4. Public Perception

The NCAA's reputation has taken a beating in recent years. Critics argue that it's out of touch, overly bureaucratic, and focused more on maintaining power than serving athletes. And while the organization has made efforts to improve its image, it's still a tough sell.

How the NCAA Is Trying to Adapt

Despite these challenges, the NCAA isn't throwing in the towel. Here's how it's trying to stay relevant in the NIL era:

1. A Push for Federal Legislation

The NCAA has been lobbying Congress for a federal NIL law that would create uniform rules across the country. While progress has been slow, the NCAA is betting big on the idea that a national framework could restore some order to the chaos.

2. Focusing on Championships

If there's one thing the NCAA still does well, it's organizing national championships. March Madness remains a cultural phenomenon, and the College World Series continues to draw huge crowds. By doubling down on its role as the steward of college sports' biggest events, the NCAA is hoping to remind everyone why it matters.

3. Strengthening Compliance

The NCAA has ramped up its compliance efforts in recent years, focusing on enforcing eligibility rules and cracking down on blatant violations. While it can't control every aspect of NIL, it's trying to ensure that the basic rules of the game are followed.

4. Embracing Change (Sort Of)

While the NCAA has been slow to adapt, it's not entirely resistant to change. The organization has started to acknowledge that athletes deserve a bigger piece of the pie and is exploring ways to modernize its approach without abandoning its core principles.

Looking Ahead

So what's next for the NCAA? The road ahead is uncertain, but a few trends are emerging:

1. **Federal Action**

    If Congress passes a federal NIL law, the NCAA could regain some control over the landscape. But if not, the patchwork of state laws will likely continue to grow, creating even more headaches for the organization.

2. **A Narrower Focus**

    The NCAA might decide to focus on what it does best - organizing championships and enforcing basic rules - while leaving the rest to schools and conferences.

3. **A New Playbook**

    To survive in the NIL era, the NCAA will need to embrace

innovation, transparency, and collaboration. Whether it's working with collectives, supporting athlete education, or finding new ways to promote fairness, the organization will need to prove that it can evolve.

A Message to the NCAA

To the NCAA: you've had a rough few years, but you're still here. The NIL era has challenged you in ways you never imagined, but it's also created opportunities to rethink your role and make college athletics better for everyone.

Yes, it's messy. Yes, it's chaotic. But remember: the joy is in the journey. And if nothing else, you've given us plenty to talk about - and laugh about - along the way.

Now, back to the game. The athletes are thriving, the fans are cheering, and the future of college sports is still being written. Let's see where it goes.

Chapter 36
The NIL Effect - Loyalty at Last?

Seasoned Veterans in College, High School Transferring Slows Down, and Shallow Pro Drafts

In the world of *No Immediate Loyalty,* where student-athletes have been seemingly free agents in the NIL era, a surprising shift is occurring in now. For the first time in years, we're seeing high school and college sports transferring and jumping to the pros prematurely settles down a bit. The days of constant transferring, chasing professional dreams, or hopping from school to school might actually be slowing - thanks to NIL itself.

Here's the new reality: the exceptional and elite high school athletes are staying put, turning down transfers because NIL opportunities and scholarships are coming to *them.* And in college, those same elite athletes are also staying loyal to their schools, reaping the benefits of NIL deals and lucrative pay at major Universities tailored to their local markets and enjoying the stability of being the face of their programs.

Meanwhile, the transfer portal is no longer the chaotic free-for-all it once was. Instead, most of the movement in college sports is coming from Division I athletes transferring down to mid-major schools for more playing time. This stability has created a new landscape of seasoned veteran rosters in college athletics - and it's having ripple effects all the way to the professional leagues, where pro drafts are suddenly less deep in talent.

High School NIL: Why the Elite Athletes Are Staying Put

In the early days of NIL, many high school athletes were transferring to states that allowed NIL deals, prep schools, powerhouse programs, or other high schools to maximize their exposure and NIL opportunities. But now, a new trend has emerged: the best athletes are staying at their original schools.

Why? Because the NIL era has flipped the script. Now, instead of athletes chasing opportunities, the opportunities are chasing the athletes.

1. **Local NIL Deals**

    Elite high school athletes are securing NIL deals with major national brands, partnering with local businesses, car dealerships, or even regional brands. Staying local means these athletes can build their personal brands while staying close to their communities - no need to transfer to a national powerhouse.

2. **Free Tuition and Scholarships**

    Some private high schools are getting creative, offering full scholarships or tuition waivers to elite athletes to keep them at their schools. In states where NIL is allowed for high school athletes, these schools are also leveraging their networks to help athletes secure sponsorships, ensuring there's no financial reason to leave...and starting NIL Collectives on the high school level!

3. **Community Loyalty**

    For many high school athletes, staying in their hometowns means maintaining their support systems - friends, family, coaches, and fans. NIL has made it profitable to stay loyal, creating a win-win for athletes and their communities.

As one high school coach joked, "In the old days, you had to beg your star player not to transfer. Now, you just introduce them to the owner of the popular local sushi or pizza chain, and they're staying put."

College Loyalty: Why the Best Athletes Aren't Transferring

In college sports, the NIL landscape is having a similar effect. The elite athletes - the ones who could transfer to any school in the country - are choosing to stay put. Here's why:

1. **Lucrative Pay from the Major D1 College Revenue-Sharing** plans adopted by the NCAA.

2. **Tailored NIL Deals**

   For star athletes, staying at the same school means more lucrative NIL deals. Local businesses, alumni networks, and school-specific collectives are investing heavily in keeping these athletes happy. Why start over somewhere else when you've already built a profitable brand at your current school?

3. **Stability and Veteran Status**

   Staying at the same school allows athletes to grow into leadership roles and become the face of their programs. This not only boosts their NIL earning potential but also prepares them for life after college - whether that's in the pros or another career.

As one college basketball player put it, "Why would I transfer when I've got a billboard in town and free burgers for life from the local diner?"

3. **Team Chemistry and Winning Programs**

    Elite athletes know that stability breeds success. By staying at their schools, they're helping their teams build chemistry and continuity - key ingredients for winning championships. And let's be real, winning is great for a personal brand.

The New Transfer Portal Trend

While the elite athletes are staying put, the transfer portal is still active - but the movement looks very different now.

1. **D1 to Mid-Majors**

    The majority of transfers are now coming from Division I athletes moving down to mid - major programs in search of more playing time. These athletes are prioritizing their on-court/on-field development over NIL earnings, recognizing that more minutes can lead to better pro prospects - or simply more enjoyment of the game.

2. **The Role of NIL for Transfers**

    Even for athletes transferring to mid-majors, NIL plays a role. Smaller schools are offering creative NIL opportunities (think partnerships with regional businesses or alumni-backed collectives) to attract talent from bigger programs.

As one mid-major coach quipped, "We're not the big fish, but we've got plenty of room in the pond. And hey, our local coffee shop makes a mean latte."

The Rise of Seasoned Veterans

This newfound loyalty among elite athletes has reshaped college sports in dramatic ways.

1. **Older, More Experienced Teams**

   With fewer athletes transferring and more players staying in college longer (thanks to NIL money easing financial pressures), college teams are now filled with seasoned veterans. Many rosters feature fifth-year seniors and even graduate students, creating a level of experience and maturity rarely seen before.

2. **Higher Quality of Play**

   The continuity and experience of these veteran teams are raising the level of competition. Games are more strategic, rivalries are fiercer, and fans love the heightened drama.

The Ripple Effect: Shallower Pro Drafts

While college sports are thriving, the professional leagues are feeling the impact of this new landscape.

1. **Fewer Early Exits**

   With NIL money providing financial security, many athletes are choosing to stay in college longer instead of declaring for the draft early. This means fewer underclassmen in the draft pools, making them shallower than in previous years.

2. **More Seasoned Rookies**

   The athletes who do declare for the draft are often older and more experienced when they enter the pros. While this can be a positive for teams looking for polished players, it also means fewer opportunities to develop raw talent.

As one NFL scout joked, "We're drafting 23-year-old rookies who've already got more NIL endorsements than our veterans."

Parting Thoughts

Writing *No Immediate Loyalty* has been an incredible journey - one filled with insights, surprises, and plenty of laughs. But more than anything, this experience has underscored just how transformative this moment is for athletes everywhere.

NIL isn't just about making money; it's about rewriting the rules, leveling the playing field, and creating opportunities that didn't exist before. It's about athletes taking charge of their futures, building their personal brands, and realizing their value both on and off the field.

To the athletes reading this: *this is your time*. Embrace it. Dream big, work hard, and take ownership of your story. Build your brand, but don't let it define you. Remember who you are, what you stand for, and the people who've supported you along the way - the ones who know you the best - do not jump to hire an agent. Your talent is your platform, but your character is your legacy.

To the parents, coaches, and mentors, the trail blazers who have adapted to this new NIL era keep rolling with the punches successfully - this is uncharted territory for everyone. Be patient, stay informed, and remember that your role is to guide, support, and empower - not to control. The athletes in your life will look to you for wisdom and encouragement, not just answers.

And to everyone else: Fans, administrators, and even skeptics: The next superstar athlete might also be the next big entrepreneur, philanthropist, or innovator. That's something worth celebrating.

For me, one thing has always been true: "*The Joy is the Journey*". Writing this book has been a journey of discovery, reflection, and connection. Thank you for joining me on this ride. The future of sports has never looked brighter - or more exciting.

Send me your thoughts and stories

Mike Ross Founder and CEO, ConNEXTions Foundation

Entrepreneur Philanthropist Author
📞 Cell: 818 - 823 - 3862

Mike@ConNEXTions.pro
✘ *Empowering Athletes - Building Futures*
🌐 Visit Us Online   www.connextions.pro

✉ *Let's build, connect, and inspire!*

No Immediate Loyalty

www.ingramcontent.com/pod-product-compliance
Lightning Source LLC
Chambersburg PA
CBHW070058080526
44586CB00013B/1115